Andree Ochoa

ONLINE MAGIC

Learn the secrets to online success.

This ebook was created with StreetLib Write

https://writeapp.io

Table of contents

DEDICATION 1

Introduction 3

Chapter 1 - Planning for the future an introduction to online presence 5

    Understanding the Importance of a Website 8

    Evolution of Online Presence 10

    Setting Goals for Your Online Presence 18

    Key Components of a Successful Website 23

    Do you have the right domain name? 29

Chapter 2 - Website Fundamentals 33

    Overview of Hosting and Servers 41

    Choosing Between DIY and Professional Web Development ... 44

    Selecting the Right Webmaster or Development Team 49

Chapter 3 - Audience Analysis 55

    Conducting Audience Research, know what your users want ... 58

    Crafting User Personas 62

    Tailoring Design and Content to Your Audience 66

Chapter 4 - Content Strategy — 71
A Tale of Protection and Compliance — 71
Crafting Compelling Call-to-Actions (CTAs) — 74
Lead Generation Strategies — 76
Maintaining a Unique and Engaging Content Strategy — 78

Chapter 5 - Design and User Experience — 83
Optimizing Website Navigation — 86
Visual Design and Branding Guidelines — 88
Accessibility Considerations for All Users — 91

Chapter 6 - Website Optimization — 95
Personalizing Online Experience — 96
Ensuring Cross-Browser Compatibility — 98
Implementing Interactive Features and Chatbots — 100
Placing Ads Strategically for Monetization — 102

Chapter 7 - Website Maintenance and Security — 105
Utilizing Maintenance Tools and Platforms — 107
Implementing Security Measures Against Cyber Threats — 112
Data Protection and Compliance Considerations — 115

Chapter 8 - Marketing Strategies — 121
Creating and Managing a Blog for Content Marketing — 133
Leveraging Offline Traditional Media for Online Success — 137

Chapter 9 - Search Engine Optimization (SEO) — 141

Implementing SEM Strategies for Visibility — 145
Building Quality Backlinks and Off-Page SEO — 150
Leveraging Social Media for SEO Benefits — 154

Chapter 10 - Monetization Tactics — 161

Exploring Diverse Monetization Methods — 164
Developing and Managing Affiliate Programs — 166
Converting Website Traffic into Sales Leads — 168
Creating and Selling Digital Products — 172
Implementing Subscription-Based Models — 175
Offering Premium Content and Memberships — 179
Monetizing Email Newsletters and Lists — 182
Hosting Webinars and Online Courses — 184
Leveraging Sponsored Content and Paid Reviews — 188
Taking payments Online — 191

Chapter 11 - Virtual Office Setup — 197

Essential Tools and Technologies for Remote Work — 200
Ensuring Productivity and Collaboration Online — 204
Overcoming Challenges of Remote Operations — 207

Chapter 12 - Performance Monitoring and Analytics — 211

Utilizing Google Analytics for Insights — 213
Alternative Analytics Tools — 216
Key Performance Indicators (KPIs) — 218
Iterative Improvements Based on Data Analysis — 222

Strategies for Continuous Optimization	224
Analytics for Security Monitoring	227
Monitoring performance conclusion	230

Chapter 13 - Conclusion ... 233

Encouragement for Ongoing Development	236
Final Thoughts on Online Magic the True Path to Success	238
Glossary	241
DISCLAIMER	247

DEDICATION

Dear reader, thank you for purchasing "Online Magic", I hope you find everything you expect to learn. You and I together will be going over many subjects and concepts that will help you learn how to create a successful online presence and make money from it.

I would like to dedicate this book to my mom and dad, and to all the people in my life who gave me the right tools and put me in the right path for me to overcome and have a good future. I'd also like to thank my many mentors for giving me advice and supporting me at different points in my life, special thanks to all my work team members who have been by my side all of these years and also to all the people around me who have believed in me and who have made this book possible.

In the following pages you will learn how to plan your website, create a successful online presence and make money using the internet combining offline and online efforts, and I will teach you the way to have a successful online presence based on my own experiences and knowledge of the internet industry, knowledge that I have acquired during the years and situations that have passed.

So, let's go and dive in to this exciting new adventure.

INTRODUCTION

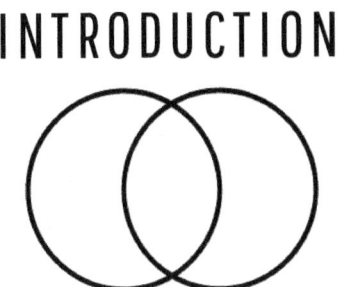

This book is intended for persons who are thinking of starting a brand-new website and for those that already own a website and want to make it better. To understand this book, you may be required little or no technical knowledge, I'll try to be as specific as I can and will try to explain everything in detail. T hroughout this book, I'll be sharing important insights and commentary. To make these key points stand out, I'll enclose them within quotation marks and present them in *italic* formatting. Keep an eye out for these remarks as they provide valuable guidance and additional context to the content presented.

The point of this book is to help you learn to create successful websites, promote and bring as much traffic as you can to your website so you can close more sales, get more leads, gain more email subscribers, or whatever other use that you may give to your website traffic. It's not just about your website being good or having a good design, it's not only about your SEO work or search engine submission. It's about all of those things together in a whole. Think about it like a football, a good football is formed with many pieces of leather all sawed together to become a ball, good websites also follow that pattern. They are all integrated by many different pieces that form a complete and successful website.

It's worth mentioning that the content in this book is based on real life experiences, and time and places as well as names have been changed to protect real identities of people.

Having said this, I would like to begin with what's important, let's not waste any more time and continue. Hope you enjoy my book and don't hesitate to contact me for more information, questions or comments at my website: https://www.andreeochoa.com

CHAPTER 1 - PLANNING FOR THE FUTURE AN INTRODUCTION TO ONLINE PRESENCE

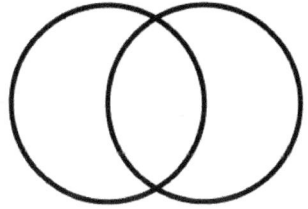

In the summer of 1998, nestled in the bustling town of Tijuana, Mexico, I found myself at a pivotal juncture. As a restless and curious child, I harbored a deep fascination for all things electronic, nurtured by my stepfather's passion for sound systems and gadgets. Despite his occasional frustration with my tinkering, it was through his influence that I was first introduced to the captivating world of electronics.

Amidst the chaos of adjusting to my mother's recent marriage and the demise of my beloved Nintendo console, I yearned for a new outlet for my boundless energy and creativity. However, fate had other plans, and instead of the coveted Super Nintendo, I found myself in possession of a SEGA system that failed to capture my imagination.

Online Magic

As the years unfolded, and after having gone to live with my dad. I embarked on a journey of self-discovery and resilience, shaped by the lessons learned within the confines of my father's furniture factory. Surrounded by sawdust and unfinished wood, I absorbed the invaluable teachings of hard work and determination, laying the groundwork for my future endeavors.

It was within this humble environment that my passion for computers was ignited, fueled by the dusty relics of my uncle and dad's antiquated PC's. Despite my limited access to technology, I immersed myself in the world of computer science, driven by an insatiable thirst for knowledge and understanding.

As the dawn of the new millennium heralded the advent of the internet age, I found myself on the cusp of a digital revolution. With companies like AOL and Yahoo offering free internet access via dial-up connections, the world wide web beckoned with untold possibilities and boundless opportunities.

However, amidst the excitement and promise of the burgeoning internet era, I remained grounded in the realities of hard work and perseverance at my father's furniture factory. Armed with newfound skills, time passing by, and a relentless determination to succeed. I then embarked on a journey of exploration and discovery, navigating the ever-changing landscape of technology with unwavering resolve. I was one of that rare breeds of people who found themselves immersed in technology in a garage or in my case in an Internet cafe with my group of friends discovering what could be achieved on the Internet. I remember that we would get together to have marathons of eating, drinking, and programming. " Those were the good old days!"

From the dusty aisles of a furniture factory, to the bustling corridors of a call center, and even navigating the vibrant atmosphere of a swap meet, my path was fraught with challenges and setbacks. Yet, with each obstacle overcome, I emerged stronger and more resilient, propelled by a steadfast belief in the transformative power of innovation and ingenuity that technology offers.

As I reflect on my journey from humble beginnings to newfound success, I am reminded of the profound impact that planning for the future and embracing the digital world can have on one's life. Through dedication, perseverance, and a willingness to adapt to changing circumstances, I have witnessed firsthand the transformative power of online presence and the boundless opportunities it affords.

As we step into a new era of technological innovation, let's welcome the boundless opportunities of the digital age with enthusiasm. By meticulously planning and looking ahead, we can tap into the potential of our online presence to carve out a brighter, more prosperous future for ourselves and future generations.

Understanding the Importance of a Website

As I started and continued to manage my IT consulting agency, I recognized the potential to expand my services into the digital world. Thus, I ventured into offering website design services, and internet connectivity within the confines of the building where I was located at the time. However, my initial foray into providing wireless internet coverage was met with challenges, limited by budget constraints.

Undeterred, I sought opportunities to enhance my network infrastructure and broaden my clientele. Securing a more affordable office space enabled me to extend my wireless internet coverage to additional buildings nearby and downtown areas. A turning point occurred when I began offering hosting co-location services to various businesses and government entities. This propelled my venture into internet sales and establishing a robust online presence.

Inspired by this newfound success, I ventured into online sales of domain names and hosting services, as well as other internet technologies. Despite initial setbacks, including domain name availability issues, I persevered in my pursuit of acquiring DomainCart.com, the cornerstone of my online venture. After years of negotiation and strategic planning, I finally secured the domain from a private seller, marking a pivotal moment in my journey.

With DomainCart.com as my platform, I set out to revolutionize the online marketplace, offering a comprehensive suite of services including domain registration, hosting, SSL certificates, and email solutions.

Driven by passion and unwavering determination, I left no stone unturned in creating a user-friendly interface and securing top-notch infrastructure to provide unmatched service to my clientele. This propelled me to seek out collaborations with leading tech giants, bonds that continue to thrive and flourish, shaping the trajectory of my journey to this very day.

Moving from an IT firm to a comprehensive internet service business marked a pivotal shift in my priorities, directing my attention toward crafting user-centric website interfaces customized to meet the distinct requirements of every client. Along this journey, I delved deeper into the intricacies of effective website design, traffic generation, lead acquisition, and sales generation. This evolution led me to immerse myself in the realm of meticulous keyword research, meticulously optimizing my website to achieve peak visibility and influence. Back in the day a few people knew how to do this, and nobody shared the information, so it was basically an everyday A/B testing task.

My journey has been marked by milestones, from whirlwind adventures from Costa Rica, Mexico, and the U.S.A., to exclusive VIP events and international fashion shows. Today, DomainCart.com stands as a beacon of innovation and excellence, offering cutting-edge solutions in internet related services.

As we continue to evolve and adapt to the ever-changing digital landscape, one thing remains clear: the importance of a website extends far beyond its aesthetics. It serves as a gateway to the digital world, a testament to your brand identity, and a powerful tool for driving growth and success.

In a world where online presence is paramount, let us embrace the transformative power of technology and leverage it to unlock new opportunities and achieve greater heights of success. Together, we can navigate the complexities of the digital world and emerge stronger, wiser, and more resilient than ever before.

Evolution of Online Presence

The evolution of online presence has been a fascinating journey marked by significant advancements in technology and changing consumer behaviors. The internet has transformed the way we communicate, interact, and do business, making it essential for individuals and businesses to establish a strong online presence. Let's explore the evolution of online presence, from the early days of the internet to the sophisticated digital landscape of today.

In the early days of the internet, online presence was a simple concept that involved creating a basic HTML website or blog to share information with others. Websites were static, text-based pages that lacked interactivity and multimedia elements. Businesses and individuals used websites primarily as online brochures or portfolios to showcase their products, services, or expertise. Most websites were operated by schools, students, government entities, or large corporations. Social interaction occurred through participation in IRC chat rooms. IRC, short for Internet Relay Chat, is often regarded as a forerunner to contemporary social networks. It operates as a protocol facilitating real-time text communication over the internet. While it may not align with the conventional concept of a social network due to its absence of user profiles and other typical social media features, to this day IRC serves as a platform for social engagement and community formation.

As the internet progressed into what we now refer to as the commercial era of web 1.0, IRC played a significant role in shaping online communication.

The emergence of social media platforms such as My Space, Hi5, AOL and MSN messenger, Facebook, Twitter, LinkedIn, Instagram and others combined with mobile access led us to what we now know as web 2.0. This revolutionized online presence by enabling individuals and businesses to connect and engage with their audiences, clients, family, and friends in real-time. Social media allowed for two-way communication, content sharing, and community building, making it easier for brands to build relationships with customers and prospects.

The proliferation of smartphones and tablets has further transformed online presence, making it imperative for websites to be mobile-friendly and responsive. Mobile devices have become the primary means of accessing the internet, prompting businesses to optimize their websites for mobile users to enhance the user experience and improve search engine rankings.

Living all that led us to an era of what I call "The E-commerce boom" which also played a crucial role in the evolution of online presence, this combined with mobile apps, brought us to what is today the web 3.0. As businesses have increasingly shifted their focus to online sales and digital marketing strategies. E-commerce platforms such as Shopify, WooCommerce, and Magento have made it easier for businesses to set up online stores, process payments, and reach global audiences.

This caused content marketing to emerged as a key component of online presence, with businesses creating and distributing valuable, relevant, and engaging content to attract and retain customers. Blogs, videos, infographics, podcasts, and social media posts have become essential tools for building brand awareness, driving website traffic, and generating leads.

All of this has made search engine optimization (SEO) and search engine marketing (SEM) become essential strategies for improving online visibility and driving organic and paid traffic to websites. Businesses invest in SEO and SEM tactics to increase their search engine rankings, boost website traffic, and generate leads and sales.

As you can see, through the evolution of the internet, establishing a strong online presence offers a range of benefits for individuals and businesses, including:

- Increased brand visibility and awareness
- Expanded reach and audience engagement
- Improved customer relationships and loyalty
- Easier access to global markets and customers
- Higher website traffic and conversions

This is why it's important to create a successful online presence. Consider the following practical tips:

- Identify your target audience and define your online goals
- Choose the right domain name and hosting provider for your website
- Design a user-friendly and visually appealing website

- Create high-quality content that is relevant and valuable to your audience
- Engage with your audience on social media and respond to feedback and questions
- Optimize your website for search engines to improve visibility and ranking
- Monitor your online presence and performance using analytics tools, and repeat.

The above list of practical tips should work for almost any type of business when starting to plan your online presence.

I've created two case studies based on real life situations that I would have liked to capture in full here, but instead I leave you a summary of them. Which I believe will serve as an example to understand the importance of online presence and where it is headed.

Case Studies

Case Study 1: Emma's Jewelry E-commerce Transformation

Facing an uphill battle for online visibility, Emma's Jewelry, a small e-commerce venture specializing in handmade jewelry, underwent a comprehensive overhaul of its digital presence. Recognizing the growing importance of mobile accessibility, Emma's revamped its website to ensure seamless navigation and functionality across various devices. The company adopted a strategic content marketing approach, emphasizing compelling storytelling and visually captivating content to engage its target audience effectively.

The results of these strategic initiatives were transformative. Emma's Jewelry experienced a remarkable 50% surge in website traffic, indicating a significant increase in online visibility and brand awareness. This surge in traffic translated directly into tangible business outcomes, with sales soaring by 30%, demonstrating a substantial boost in revenue generation. Additionally, Emma's witnessed a notable 20% expansion in its social media following, indicating enhanced audience engagement and brand affinity across digital platforms.

The success of Emma's Jewelry e-commerce transformation serves as a testament to the power of strategic digital marketing initiatives tailored to meet the evolving needs and preferences of today's online consumers. Through a combination of website optimization, content marketing excellence, and a customer-centric approach, Emma's not only enhanced its online presence but also achieved measurable growth in sales and brand engagement, positioning itself for sustained success in the competitive e-commerce landscape.

Case Study 2: Jane's Journey to Freelance Writing Succes

Jane, a talented freelance writer, embarked on her professional journey with a vision to establish a thriving online presence and carve a niche for herself in the competitive world of freelance writing. Leveraging the power of digital platforms, Jane set out to create a robust online portfolio that would showcase her writing prowess, expertise, and unique voice.

Central to Jane's strategy was the development of a personal website that served as a dynamic hub for her professional endeavors. Through her website, Jane meticulously curated an extensive writing portfolio, showcasing a diverse range of projects, articles, and creative works that highlighted her versatility and skill set. Additionally, Jane maintained an active blog where she shared industry insights, writing tips, and personal reflections, further demonstrating her thought leadership and expertise in the field.

In parallel, Jane recognized the importance of social media as a powerful tool for networking and audience engagement. By strategically leveraging platforms like LinkedIn, Twitter, and Instagram, Jane cultivated a vibrant online presence, engaging with her audience, participating in relevant discussions, and sharing valuable content that resonated with her target audience. Moreover, Jane actively collaborated with fellow writers, bloggers, and industry influencers, fostering meaningful connections and expanding her professional network.

The results of Jane's strategic approach were nothing short of remarkable. Armed with a compelling online portfolio and a robust social media presence, Jane successfully attracted new clients, garnered writing gigs, and secured lucrative opportunities within her industry. Additionally, Jane's proactive engagement with her audience and her commitment to delivering high-quality content positioned her as a trusted authority in the freelance writing community, further enhancing her reputation and credibility.

Jane's journey serves as a testament to the transformative power of a strategic and multifaceted approach to building an online presence. Through her dedication, creativity, and relentless pursuit of excellence, Jane not only achieved success as a freelance writer but also paved the way for continued growth and expansion in her professional endeavors.

As you can see, having a good online presence can greatly influence how our business performs. I have witnessed firsthand the evolution of online presence and the impact it has on businesses and individuals. Through my personal and professional experiences, I have learned the importance of establishing a strong online presence, engaging with your target audience, and continuously optimizing your digital assets to stay ahead in today's competitive online landscape.

The evolution of online presence has come a long way from static websites to dynamic social media platforms, e-commerce stores, and content-rich blogs. By embracing the latest digital trends and technologies, individuals and businesses can create a successful online presence that drives brand awareness, customer engagement, and revenue growth. Online magic is within reach for those who are willing to invest time, effort, and resources in building and maintaining their online presence.

Setting Goals for Your Online Presence

Recognizing the importance of establishing clear objectives for your online presence, I aim to elucidate effective strategies for meticulously planning and attaining success in the digital landscape. Leveraging my extensive background in IT and proficiency in digital marketing, I endeavor to offer invaluable insights derived from years of nurturing my online presence and driving revenue through various online avenues.

Setting goals for your online presence is crucial for achieving success in the digital world. Without clear objectives and a roadmap to guide your efforts, it's easy to get lost in the vast expanse of the internet. Let me share some insights I have gathered throughout my journey, focusing on how to plan your website, create a successful online presence, and ultimately make money online.

"Know Your Purpose"

Before diving deeper into the world of online presence, it's essential to define your purpose. Understanding why you want to establish an online presence will help guide your decision-making process and ensure that your efforts are aligned with your goals. Whether you aim to build a personal brand, sell products or services, or share valuable content with a specific audience, having a clear purpose will set the tone for your online presence.

Once you've clarified your purpose, it's time to visualize your website's future. Envision how you want it to look, feel, and function. Consider the user experience: How will visitors navigate your site? What actions do you want them to take? Close your eyes and imagine the unique features and elements that will set your website apart from the competition. Also, imagine that you're already using your website —How does it feel? Picture yourself effortlessly managing your online sales and interacting with customers as if your website already exists. By vividly imagining your website's desired outcome and actively engaging with this vision, you'll lay the foundation for a successful development journey.

You should start by identifying your target audience which is crucial for crafting a successful online presence. By understanding who your audience is, their needs, preferences, and behaviors, you can tailor your content, messaging, and marketing strategies to resonate with them effectively. Conducting market research, analyzing data, and engaging with your audience will help you create a connection that drives engagement, loyalty, and ultimately, conversions.

Also, like everything in life, it is important to set goals. When setting goals for your online presence, it's essential to follow the SMART criteria – Specific, Measurable, Achievable, Relevant, and Time-bound. By establishing clear, quantifiable objectives, you can track your progress, measure success, and make adjustments as needed.

Whether your goals involve increasing website traffic, generating leads, or boosting conversion rates, ensuring they are SMART will give you a solid foundation for growth.

Take a look at the following example table of smart goals that was done for Emma's Jewelry when her new website was planned.

Emma's Jewelry Table of SMART Goals

| Goal | Key Metrics | Target | Dead- |

			line
Increase Website Traffic	Unique Visitors, Page Views	20% Growth	Q3 2022
Improve Conversion Rate	Conversion Rate	5% Increase	Q4 2022
Expand Email Subscriber List	Subscribers	1,000 Subs	Q2 2022

Once your SMART goals have been set you can continue on your journey. But first let's explore the following three topics in a summarized way.

Develop a Content Strategy

Content is king in the online world, and having a robust content strategy is essential for building a successful online presence. Whether you create blog posts, videos, podcasts, or social media content, consistency is key. Define your content pillars, voice, tone, and cadence to ensure that your messaging aligns with your brand and resonates with your audience.

Set dates for posting/uploading content to your website and do so in an orderly manner so your users can relate to your regular updates. Reflect yourself or your experience in your content or updates and ask yourself if your customers are getting the information they need from your website. Make use of analytics tools to track performance and optimize your content strategy for maximum impact.

Leverage SEO and Digital Marketing

Search engine optimization (SEO) and digital marketing are invaluable tools for driving traffic to your website and increasing visibility online. By optimizing your website for search engines, implementing keyword strategies, and creating compelling content, you can improve your organic search rankings and attract relevant traffic. Additionally, investing in digital marketing channels such as social media, email marketing, and pay-per-click advertising can help you reach a broader audience and drive conversions.

Monetize Your Online Presence

Once you have established a strong online presence, it's time to monetize your efforts. There are various ways to generate income online, including affiliate marketing, sponsored content, selling products or services, and creating digital products. Evaluate your options, experiment with different monetization strategies, and track performance to identify what works best for your audience and aligns with your goals.

Establishing clear goals for your online presence lays the foundation for a thriving digital journey. From clarifying your purpose to identifying your target audience and crafting SMART goals, each step plays a pivotal role in shaping your success. However, while SMART goals provide a tangible framework for progress, it's essential to recognize the value of other objectives that may be less measurable but equally significant. Goals such as fostering community engagement, content strategies, search engine optimization (SEO), monetizing, and upholding brand integrity contribute to the holistic growth and sustainability of your online presence. By embracing a balanced approach that encompasses both measurable and qualitative goals, you can cultivate a dynamic and impactful digital presence that resonates with your audience and drives long-term success.

"Remember that success in the online world takes time, effort, and perseverance."

Key Components of a Successful Website

Making your website successful is crucial for individuals and businesses looking to establish an online presence and make money. I have spent years perfecting the art of creating successful websites that generate income. Let me share with you the key components that are essential for a website to succeed in the competitive online world.

Like I mentioned in the past chapter, before you even start building your website, it's crucial to have a clear understanding of its purpose and target audience. What is the goal of your website? Who are you trying to reach? Does it reflect yourself and/or experience? Without a defined purpose and target audience, your website will lack direction and may not attract the right visitors. Condemning it to not bring the results you are looking for. So, it's important to always plan what you want your audience to find in your website before starting your development.

In today's mobile-first world, having a responsive design is essential for a successful website. This means that your website should be able to adapt to different screen sizes and devices, providing users with a seamless browsing experience whether they are using a desktop computer, tablet, or smartphone. Keep in mind it's not mandatory to always show the same information in your mobile website than in your desktop version. Some companies choose to only show the important parts or tools of their websites in the mobile version due to the lack of screen space in some devices. To know how to choose what to show you can always rely on your website analytics to look for your most visited content.

"Always test your website in different screen sizes both desktop and in mobile versions."

After your design is fully tested, is now time to think about the content. Content is king when it comes to driving traffic to your website and engaging visitors. High-quality, relevant content that is optimized for search engines will not only attract more visitors but also keep them coming back for more. From blog posts to videos to infographics, make sure your content is informative, engaging, and valuable to your audience. The same way content is made for your social media accounts in a daily basis, it needs to be made for your website. And it is best if your social media content approach matches your website. I'm not saying is mandatory to update your website on a daily basis, but if you do it will definitely help your search engine rankings.

Another important aspect for the proper functioning of a website it's that it has to have a user-friendly navigation. A website with confusing navigation can quickly turn off visitors and make them abandon your site. Ensure that your website has a clear, intuitive navigation menu that makes it easy for users to find what they are looking for. Consider organizing your content into categories and sub-categories to help users navigate your site more effectively. Also make sure you always give priority link placement to important links such as the product or service you want to sell, your contact page or phone number, basically your main call-to-action, or the most visited pages of your website. When choosing what's important for your menu you can always rely on your website analytics to view which pages are performing best.

An effective call-to-action (CTA) shown in the right spot serves as a powerful tool in transforming visitors into valuable leads or customers. Whether it involves subscribing to a newsletter, completing a purchase, or reaching out for further information, your website ought to feature distinct and persuasive CTAs that motivate visitors to engage with your offerings. Simply put, a call-to-action guides users towards the specific action you want them to take, driving conversions and advancing your business objectives. It's not that hard, don't worry, we will dive deeper in to call-to-actions in the following chapters.

However, because we now live in a fast-paced world, no one has time to wait for a slow-loading website. Make sure your website loads quickly to provide users with a smooth browsing experience. Choose the right hosting server provider and hosting plan, compress images, optimize code, and leverage browser caching to improve your website's loading speed. You can always use Googles PageSpeed tools (https://developers.google.com/speed) to help you analyze and optimize your website. Website speed is really important, especially when there's competition in your business niche. A slow website could be the reason why a search engine's algorithm would decide to show the competition and not you.

For search engine result purposes, it's not just website speed, but also Search Engine Optimization (SEO) which is a crucial component of a successful website, as it helps improve your site's visibility in search engine results pages. From keyword optimization to meta tags to backlink building, make sure your website is optimized for search engines to attract more organic traffic. To SEO optimize your website means to make your website easy to read and understand for search engine robots so they can in turn refer as many traffic as they can back to your website when their users search their portals for information. Like Google there are other important search engines out there for example Bing, Yahoo, Yandex, DuckDuckGO, Baidu, Ask.com and many more. It's important to optimize for all of them, although almost all of them follow the same optimization pattern.

To measure the success of your website and make data-driven decisions, it's important to implement analytics and tracking tools. Platforms like Google Analytics, Matomo, Piwik PRO, Clicky, Heap, and Clarity from Microsoft provide valuable insights into how users interact with your site, which pages are performing well, and where there is room for improvement. There are many alternatives to use for analytics so make sure you use the best option for your business. Implementing analytics and tracking is easy most platforms will provide you with a piece of code you can copy and paste in your websites coding.

Professional design and branding for your website is also a very important part. A well-designed website with cohesive branding elements can help establish credibility and trust with your audience. Invest in professional design services to create a visually appealing website that reflects your brand identity and resonates with your target audience. Without forgetting the interactive part, and of course the security.

With cyber threats on the rise, prioritizing website security is paramount. It's crucial to implement measures such as SSL certification, regular backups, and robust password protection to fortify your website against potential breaches and safeguard the sensitive data of your users. Optionally encrypting your database can offer heightened security in the event of a website breach. However, it's important to strike a balance, as while an encrypted database adds an extra layer of protection, it can lead to longer load times and increased server workload. Therefore, it's crucial to carefully consider these factors when constructing your website.

By implementing these key components, you can set your website up for success and maximize its potential to generate income online. Remember, creating a successful website is an ongoing process that requires continuous optimization and adaptation to meet the ever-changing demands of the digital world.

> *"With the right strategy and a commitment to excellence, you can turn your website into a profitable online venture."*

Do you have the right domain name?

Choosing the right domain name is crucial for establishing your online identity, much like selecting the perfect storefront sign for a physical business. Your domain name is the web address that users will type into their browsers to access your website. It's your online brand, so it's essential to choose wisely. Typically, a domain name consists of two parts: the actual name (e.g., "example") and the domain extension (e.g., ".com"). The domain extension, also known as a top-level domain (TLD), is the suffix that follows the domain name and indicates the type or category of website it represents. The most common and widely recognized domain extension is .COM, but there are numerous other options available, including .NET, .ORG, .INSURE, and many more. Each extension carries its own connotations and may be more suitable for specific types of businesses or organizations. It's essential to research and consider your options carefully before making a decision. As you explore different domain name options, consider registering your domain with a reputable registrar like DomainCart.com. As a trusted domain registrar, DomainCart.com offers a wide range of domain extensions and provides essential services like domain management and support to help you establish and maintain your online presence with ease.

Here are some key considerations to keep in mind when deciding on a domain name:

1. Reflect Your Brand:

- **Business Name:** Ideally, your domain name should align with your business name or brand identity. This helps establish consistency across your marketing channels.
- **Memorability:** Choose a domain name that is easy to remember and type. Avoid complex spellings, hyphens, or numbers that could confuse potential visitors. Unless you are prepared to spend marketing dollars in to teaching your customers how to write/type your domain name.

2. Keyword Relevance:

- **Keyword Integration:** Incorporating relevant keywords into your domain name can enhance its visibility in search engine results. Identify the primary keywords related to your business or niche and consider incorporating them into your domain.
- **Product or Service Focus:** If your business name isn't available as a domain, prioritize keywords related to your products or services. For example, if you sell shoes, consider domain options like "shoesonline.com" or "buyshoesonline.com."

3. Explore Domain Extensions:

- **Beyond .COM:** While securing a .COM domain is often preferred, don't overlook alternative domain extensions like .NET, .ORG, .ME, .SHOES, or others. These extensions can offer unique branding opportunities and may be more readily available than .COM domains.
- **Country-Specific Extensions:** If your target audience is primarily located in a specific country, consider using country code top-level domains (ccTLDs) like .MX for Mexico, .CO for Colombia, or .IN for India. These extensions can help localize your website and improve visibility in regional search results.

4. Consider SEO Implications:

- **Search Engine Relevance:** Search engines consider domain names when determining relevance in search results. While domain extensions play a role, factors like website content, SEO optimization, and backlinks are equally important.
- **Geotargeting:** Country-specific domain extensions can be advantageous for geotargeting purposes. If you're aiming to attract visitors from a specific region, using a relevant ccTLD can signal your website's relevance to local searchers.

5. Evaluate Availability and Competition:

- **Domain Availability:** Conduct thorough research to ensure your desired domain name is available for registration. Consider using DomainCart.com domain search tool to check availability and explore alternative options if your preferred choice is taken.

- **Competition Analysis:** Assess the competitiveness of potential domain names by researching existing websites with similar names or keywords. Avoid selecting a domain that closely resembles an established competitor's brand to prevent confusion among users.

Choosing the right domain name requires careful consideration of brand identity, keyword relevance, domain extensions, SEO implications, and competition analysis. By prioritizing these factors and conducting thorough research, you can secure a domain name that strengthens your online presence and facilitates your business objectives.

Additionally, if your domain name is not available, it may be possible to buy it from a private seller, you should also consider this as an option. Most domain registrars offer broker services to acquire domain names that are already registered.

CHAPTER 2 - WEBSITE FUNDAMENTALS

Defining a Website and Its Functionality

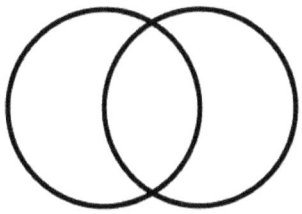

In the digital landscape of the 21st century, a website stands as a beacon of connectivity, a virtual gateway through which businesses, organizations, and individuals can reach out and connect with the world. Imagine it as a bustling marketplace, teeming with activity and opportunity, where ideas are exchanged, products are showcased, and relationships are forged. At its core, a website is more than just a collection of web pages, it's a dynamic entity that embodies the essence of its creator's vision and purpose.

Picture this: You're a budding entrepreneur with a revolutionary idea, eager to share it with the world. You envision your website as more than just an online storefront; it's a digital manifestation of your passion and ambition, a platform where you can engage with your audience and showcase your offerings in the best possible light. From the sleek design of your homepage to the seamless navigation of your product pages, every aspect of your website is carefully crafted to captivate and compel your visitors.

As you embark on your website-building journey, you'll encounter a myriad of choices and considerations. What content management system will you use to power your site? How will you design your user interface to ensure a seamless browsing experience? What functionality will you incorporate to enhance usability and engagement? These are just a few of the questions you'll need to answer as you navigate the intricate landscape of web development. But fear not, armed with the right knowledge and tools, you'll soon be well on your way to creating a website that not only meets but exceeds your wildest expectations.

Establishing an online presence has become indispensable for individuals and businesses alike, facilitating connections with their intended audience and fostering revenue generation. But what exactly constitutes a website, and how does it function? In this section, we'll explore the essence of a website and the range of functionalities it brings to the digital table.

In essence, a website serves as a digital hub comprising interconnected web pages accessible over the internet. It operates as a virtual storefront, welcoming visitors to explore a plethora of information, products, and services.

The scope and complexity of a website can vary significantly based on its objectives and the preferences of its target demographic. From straightforward static sites to dynamic, interactive platforms, the diversity in website design and functionality is vast. Let's delve deeper into the fundamental technical components that underpin the structure and operation of a website.

Explore the following table to learn the basic technical components of a website.

Technical Components of a Website

Domain Name	*This is the unique address that visitors use to access a website.*
Web Hosting	*This is the service that allows your website to be stored and accessible on the internet.*

Content Management System (CMS)	*This is the platform used to create, edit, and manage the content on your website. Popular CMS options include WordPress, Joomla, and Drupal, each offering different features and functionalities to suit your needs.*
Design and Layout	*The visual appearance of your website plays a crucial role in attracting and engaging visitors. A professional, user-friendly design with clear navigation and responsive layout is essential for a positive user experience.*
Mobile Responsiveness	*With the increasing use of smartphones and tablets, it's vital for a website to be mobile-responsive, meaning it adapts to different screen sizes and devices.*

In the world of website functionality, where each type of website serves a unique purpose and offers a distinct experience to its visitors.

Imagine strolling through the bustling streets of the internet, where websites beckon with promises of knowledge, products, and connections. As we navigate this digital landscape, we encounter websites of various types, each designed to fulfill specific needs and desires.

First, let's step into the realm of informational websites, where businesses showcase their offerings like gleaming storefronts on a busy boulevard. These websites act as virtual brochures or portfolios, providing visitors with essential information about products, services, and the company itself. With their static nature, these sites offer a glimpse into the essence of a business without the need for frequent updates.

Next, we venture into the dynamic realm of e-commerce websites, where the air is charged with excitement and anticipation. Here, visitors can peruse an array of products and services, adding items to their digital carts with a mere click of a button. Payment gateways seamlessly facilitate transactions, transforming virtual browsing into tangible purchases and deliveries.

As we continue our exploration, we stumble upon the vibrant world of blogging, where words dance across the screen like poetry in motion. Blogs are platforms for storytelling, knowledge sharing, and community building, offering a space for writers to express themselves and engage with readers through articles, stories, and posts.

Our journey takes an interactive turn as we immerse ourselves in the realm of social networking sites. Here, users connect, converse, and collaborate in a digital ecosystem teeming with text, images, and videos. From Facebook's social circles to Twitter's trending topics, these websites foster connections and conversations that transcend geographical boundaries.

Moving forward, we encounter membership-based websites, where exclusive content and services await behind virtual velvet ropes. Users must sign up and create accounts to access premium features, unlocking a world of specialized content, services, or communities. Through subscription fees, these websites offer a source of recurring revenue while providing value to their members.

Finally, we arrive at the digital classrooms of online learning websites, where knowledge is the currency and curiosity are the compass. Here, users embark on educational journeys, navigating courses, tutorials, and resources to acquire new skills and insights. Learning management systems like Moodle and Canvas serve as gateways to a world of lifelong learning and personal growth.

In this vast and diverse landscape of website functionality, each type of website plays a vital role in shaping our online experiences and fulfilling our digital needs. As we continue to explore and engage with these digital destinations, let us embrace the endless possibilities they offer and the transformative power they hold.

Let me share with you the captivating tale of how I uncovered the fundamental principles of making money online, transforming my digital presence into a lucrative source of income.

At a point in my life, I found myself standing at the crossroads of opportunity, eager to embark on a journey into online entrepreneurship. With dreams of financial freedom and creative fulfillment dancing in my mind, I set out to explore the myriad ways to monetize my website and turn my passion into profit.

As I delved deeper into the labyrinth of online business strategies, I stumbled upon the first cornerstone of monetization: advertising. Through platforms like Google AdSense, I discovered the power of displaying targeted ads on my website, opening the door to a steady stream of passive income. With each click and impression, I witnessed the potential of turning digital real estate into revenue.

But my quest for online prosperity didn't end there. With the guidance of seasoned entrepreneurs and digital mavens, I uncovered the secrets of affiliate marketing. By forging partnerships with brands and promoting their products or services on my site, I unlocked a new realm of earning potential. With every sale or referral generated through my affiliate links, I reveled in the thrill of earning a commission and building mutually beneficial relationships with trusted partners.

As my journey continued, I ventured into the realm of e-commerce, where I transformed my website into a bustling marketplace teeming with products and services. With the help of intuitive online store platforms, I curated an enticing array of offerings, inviting visitors to browse, purchase, and experience the joys of online shopping firsthand. With each transaction completed, I celebrated another step towards financial independence and business success.

But perhaps the most rewarding chapter of my journey unfolded when I embraced the power of sponsored content. By partnering with brands and influencers, I had the opportunity to create authentic, engaging content that resonated with my audience while generating revenue through sponsored posts, reviews, and endorsements. With each collaboration, I discovered the art of storytelling and the impact of genuine connections in the digital sphere.

And finally, as I gazed upon the horizon of online entrepreneurship, I realized the transformative potential of membership subscriptions. By offering premium content, services, or features to members willing to invest in exclusive access, I cultivated a loyal community of supporters and patrons, each contributing to the growth and sustainability of my digital empire.

In this grand adventure of making money online, I discovered that the fundamentals of success lie not only in the strategies we employ but also in the passion, creativity, and perseverance we bring to our endeavors. As I continue to navigate the ever-evolving landscape of digital commerce, I remain steadfast in my commitment to innovation, collaboration, and the relentless pursuit of my dreams.

Overview of Hosting and Servers

Choosing the right hosting provider and server setup is an important decision when establishing your online presence. With numerous companies offering domain registration, hosting, and email services, navigating this landscape can be overwhelming. Let's explore the key factors to consider when selecting a hosting provider and understanding server functionality.

Selecting a Domain Registrar:

1. **Established Reputation:** Opt for a reputable domain registrar with a proven track record of reliability and security. Ensure they offer competitive registration prices for your desired domain name extension (.COM, .NET, etc.).
2. **Domain Control:** Maintain full control of your domain name by registering it through a top-level regis-

trar. Avoid purchasing domains from hosting-only companies or unfamiliar entities to prevent potential loss or complications in the future.
3. **Recommended Registrar:** Consider reliable domain registrars like DomainCart.com, GoDaddy, and Network Solutions renowned for their longevity and quality services. While other options exist, choosing a trusted registrar ensures peace of mind and reliable support.

Factors to Consider When Choosing Hosting:

1. **Storage Space:** Assess the amount of hard drive space provided by the hosting company. Basic plans typically offer 10GB, suitable for most websites. However, anticipate future growth and ensure scalability for accommodating increased content and media files.
2. **Bandwidth Allocation:** Look for hosting providers offering at least 15GB of monthly bandwidth transfer. Sufficient bandwidth prevents website downtime due to exceeded traffic limits, ensuring seamless accessibility for visitors.
3. **FTP Access:** Verify that your hosting plan includes FTP access, essential for uploading and managing website files. FTP enables efficient file transfer between your computer and the hosting server, facilitating site maintenance and updates.
4. **Language Support:** Ensure your hosting plan supports HTML and PHP languages, fundamental for

website development and functionality. PHP, in particular, is indispensable for dynamic web applications and e-commerce functionalities.

5. **Email Services:** Evaluate email features, including the number of accounts provided and storage capacity. Ensure support for POP and SMTP access, enabling efficient email management and compatibility with external clients like Microsoft Outlook.
6. **Database Compatibility:** If your website requires database functionality, confirm support for databases like MySQL and MSSQL. Databases are vital for applications such as e-commerce platforms and dynamic content management systems.
7. **Pricing Structure:** While pricing is a crucial consideration, prioritize value over cost. Go for medium-tier hosting plans ($6.99 to $19.99 per month), offering ample resources for website growth and scalability. Unless you are building an app or custom software where you will need a full server, most medium hosting plans will work for your starter project.

Choosing the right hosting provider and server configuration is critical for establishing a robust online presence. By selecting a reputable domain registrar and evaluating hosting features comprehensively, you can ensure optimal performance, security, and scalability for your website. Prioritize reliability, flexibility, and future-proofing when making hosting decisions, laying a solid foundation for your digital endeavors.

"Scan the QR code below to explore the diverse range of services and products available at domaincart.com!"

Choosing Between DIY and Professional Web Development

Whether you're a small startup, a growing business, or an established brand, your website is often the first point of contact for potential customers. But when it comes to developing a website, one of the biggest decisions you'll have to make is whether to go the DIY (do-it-yourself) route or hire a professional web developer. Let's explore the pros and cons of each option to help you make an informed decision that aligns with your goals and budget.

Considering the DIY route for web development? Whether you're a budding entrepreneur, a small business owner, or simply passionate about creating your online presence, DIY web development offers both pros and cons worth considering.

Pros:

1. **Cost-effective:** One of the most appealing aspects of DIY web development is its affordability. By utilizing website builders like WordPress, Wix, Squarespace, or DomainCart.com website builder, you can create a website without breaking the bank. With options ranging from free plans to low-cost monthly subscriptions, DIY solutions offer accessible entry points for individuals and businesses alike.
2. **Full Creative Control:** When you take the reins of your website's development, you're granted total creative freedom. From selecting templates and designing layouts to crafting content, you have the autonomy to shape every aspect of your site. This level of control allows you to tailor your website to perfectly align with your brand's identity and vision.
3. **Learning Opportunity:** Embarking on a DIY web development journey isn't just about building a website—it's also a valuable learning experience. As you navigate through website builders or delve into coding languages like HTML, CSS, and JavaScript, you acquire new skills and knowledge that can prove invaluable for future projects and endeavors.

Cons:

1. **Time-consuming:** Building a website from scratch demands a significant investment of time and effort, particularly for those new to web development. Whether you're grappling with the intricacies of website builders or grappling with custom coding, the learning curve can be steep. Expect to dedicate hours to mastering tools and techniques before achieving your desired results.
2. **Limited Functionality:** While website builders offer convenience and ease of use, they may come with limitations in terms of functionality. Advanced features and customizations often require additional coding or integration, which can pose challenges for DIY developers. Without the expertise to implement complex solutions, you may find your website lacking the sophistication needed to drive engagement and conversions.
3. **Lack of Technical Support:** When technical issues arise during DIY web development, you're left to troubleshoot and resolve them independently. Without access to dedicated support teams or professional assistance, tackling bugs and glitches can be daunting. Unless you possess the necessary expertise, resolving technical challenges may prove time-consuming and frustrating.

For those ready to embark on their DIY web development journey, DomainCart.com Website Builder offers a comprehensive solution. With intuitive drag-and-drop interfaces, customizable templates, and robust features, DomainCart.com empowers users to bring their website visions to life with ease. Feel free to explore their website at (https://app.domaincart.com/products/website-builder) and take the first step towards building your online presence on your terms.

On the other hand, professional web development involves hiring a skilled web developer or web development agency to build your website for you. Here are some factors to consider if you're considering hiring a professional:

Pros:

1. **Expertise and experience:** Professional web developers have the knowledge and expertise to create high-quality, responsive websites that are optimized for performance and user experience.
2. **Customization and scalability:** A professional web developer can create a custom website tailored to your specific needs and goals. They can also ensure that your website is scalable and able to grow with your business.
3. **Technical support and maintenance:** Professional web developers provide ongoing technical support and maintenance to ensure that your website is up-to-date, secure, and functioning properly.

Cons:

1. **Cost:** Hiring a professional web developer can be expensive, especially for small businesses or startups with limited budgets. Prices can vary depending on the complexity of the project and the scope of work.
2. **Communication challenges:** Working with a professional web developer requires clear communication and ongoing collaboration. Misunderstandings or delays in communication can impact the project timeline and deliverables.
3. **Dependence on third-party:** When you hire a professional web developer, you are placing your trust in their skills and expertise. If they are unavailable or unable to fulfill their obligations, it can be challenging to find a replacement quickly.

Choosing between DIY and professional web development is a decision that should be based on your specific needs, goals, and resources. If you have the time, skills, and creativity to build a website yourself, DIY web development can be a rewarding experience that allows you to create a customized online presence. However, if you prioritize expertise, quality, and technical support, hiring a professional web developer may be the best option for you.

"Ultimately, the key to success lies in connecting with your audience and planning your website carefully, with the right approach and mindset."

Selecting the Right Webmaster or Development Team

A well-designed website is the cornerstone of that online presence, and finding the right webmaster or development team to bring your vision to life is essential. Let's go through some of the key factors to consider when selecting the right webmaster or development team for your website.

When looking for a webmaster or development team, it's important to assess their technical expertise. Make sure they are proficient in the latest web technologies, coding languages (Such as: HTML, CSS, PHP, JavaScript), and frameworks relevant to your project. A skilled webmaster will be able to optimize your website for design, speed, performance, and user experience.

Reviewing the webmaster's portfolio and/or past projects is a great way to gauge their experience and capabilities. Look for projects similar to yours in terms of scope and complexity. A webmaster with a diverse portfolio demonstrates adaptability and proficiency in handling various types of projects. Combined with effective communication, which is key to a successful web development project. The webmaster or development team should be able to clearly understand your vision, goals, and requirements. Additionally, they should provide regular updates on the progress of the project and be responsive to your feedback and questions.

Make sure the webmaster or team fully understands search engine optimization (SEO) that is crucial for driving organic traffic to your website. A knowledgeable webmaster or development team should have a good understanding of SEO best practices and be able to implement them throughout the website design and development process.

Here are some key questions you can ask a webmaster to assess their understanding of SEO along with their possible answers. Since everyone's point of view or knowledge may be different, the answers will most likely vary, but these are here to guide you.

1. **Can you explain what SEO (Search Engine Optimization) is and why it's important for websites?** SEO is the practice of optimizing websites to improve their visibility and ranking on search engine results pages (SERPs). It's important because it helps websites attract organic (unpaid) traffic, increase visibility, and reach their target audience.
2. **How do you approach keyword research for website content?** Keyword research involves identifying rele-

vant search terms and phrases that users are likely to enter into search engines when looking for information related to your website's content. Tools like Google Keyword Planner or SEMrush can be used to find keywords with high search volume and low competition.

3. **What on-page SEO factors do you consider when optimizing web pages?** On-page SEO factors include optimizing meta tags (title tags, meta descriptions), using relevant keywords in headings and content, optimizing images with descriptive alt text, ensuring a user-friendly URL structure, and improving website speed and mobile responsiveness.

4. **How do you handle meta tags, including title tags and meta descriptions?** Meta tags, such as title tags and meta descriptions, are crucial for SEO. The title tag should accurately describe the content of the web page and include relevant keywords. Meta descriptions provide a brief summary of the page's content and can influence click-through rates from search engine results.

5. **What strategies do you use for building backlinks to a website?** Building backlinks involves acquiring links from other websites to your own. Strategies include creating high-quality content that others want to link to, guest posting on relevant websites, reaching out to industry influencers for collaborations, and participating in online communities and forums.

6. **Can you explain the importance of website speed and mobile optimization for SEO?** Website speed and mobile optimization are important for SEO because search engines prioritize fast-loading, mobile-friendly websites. This improves user experience and reduces bounce rates, contributing to higher rankings on SERPs. Optimizing images, using responsive design, and minimizing code and scripts can help improve website speed and mobile performance.
7. **How do you monitor and measure the performance of SEO efforts?** Monitoring SEO performance involves tracking key metrics such as organic traffic, keyword rankings, backlink profile, and user engagement metrics like bounce rate and time on page. Tools like Google Analytics, Google Search Console, and third-party SEO platforms can provide insights into website performance and areas for improvement.
8. **Have you ever dealt with SEO penalties, and if so, how did you address them?** SEO penalties can occur when a website violates search engine guidelines, such as using black hat SEO tactics or engaging in spammy link-building practices. Addressing penalties involves identifying and removing low-quality or spammy content, disavowing toxic backlinks, and submitting a reconsideration request to the search engine.
9. **What are your thoughts on the role of content quality and relevance in SEO?** Content quality and relevance are crucial for SEO because search engines aim

to deliver the most relevant and valuable content to users. High-quality content that is informative, well-written, and relevant to user intent is more likely to rank well on SERPs and attract organic traffic.

10. **Can you share examples of successful SEO campaigns or improvements you've implemented in the past?** Successful SEO campaigns involve a combination of technical optimization, content creation, and strategic link building. Examples include improving website speed and mobile responsiveness, creating comprehensive and authoritative content, optimizing meta tags and on-page elements, and building a diverse backlink profile from reputable sources.

Before enlisting the services of a webmaster or development team, it's crucial to have an open discussion about your budget and the timeframe for the project. Gain a thorough understanding of the associated costs and the projected timeline for project completion. Keep in mind that entrusting your project to a skilled webmaster or development team is a direct investment in the long-term success of your online venture.

Moreover, it's imperative to recognize that a website is not a one-time endeavor; rather, it necessitates continuous support and maintenance to uphold its optimal functionality. Therefore, it's advisable to engage in conversations regarding post-launch support and ongoing maintenance with the selected webmaster or development team. Considering the option of signing a maintenance contract can provide assurance that your website will receive consistent updates and security measures, ensuring its sustained performance and resilience.

Don't hesitate to ask for references or read reviews from past clients. Hearing about other clients' experiences can give you valuable insights into the webmaster's work ethic, professionalism, and the quality of their work.

Selecting the right webmaster or development team is not a difficult task but rather an important step in creating a successful online presence for your business. By considering factors such as technical expertise, portfolio, communication skills, SEO knowledge, budget, timeline, support, and maintenance, you can ensure that your website is in capable hands. Remember, a well-designed website is not just a digital storefront, but a powerful tool that can help you reach your business goals and make money online. With the right webmaster or development team by your side, the possibilities are endless.

Choose your webmaster or development team wisely, and watch your online presence thrive. Feel free to reach out to me and my team any time through AndreeOchoa.com. We're here to assist you!

CHAPTER 3 - AUDIENCE ANALYSIS

Identifying Your Target Audience

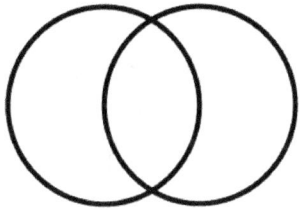

Identifying your target audience for a website can be a time-consuming and technical task. It involves not only defining the demographics and psychographics of your audience but also understanding their behaviors, preferences, and pain points. Additionally, crafting user personas based on this research can provide valuable insights into the needs and desires of your target audience, guiding the design of user experiences and the implementation of marketing strategies that resonate with your intended users. Here are several steps to effectively identify your target audience:

1. **Define Your Website's Purpose:** Like I explained in past chapters of this book. Begin by clarifying the pri-

mary goal of your website. Determine whether it's informational, transactional (e-commerce), educational, entertainment-focused, or serves another purpose. Understanding your website's objectives will help shape your target audience profile. Not that you can't change it later, but is best if you start with the right approach.

2. **Conduct Market Research:** Conduct thorough market research to gather insights into your industry, competitors, and potential audience demographics. Utilize online surveys, interviews, focus groups, and social media analytics to collect valuable data.

3. **Create Buyer Personas:** Develop detailed buyer personas representing your ideal customers. Consider demographic factors such as age, gender, location, income level, occupation, education, and marital status. Additionally, explore psychographic attributes like interests, hobbies, values, lifestyle, attitudes, and pain points.

4. **Analyze Existing Customers:** Analyze data from your existing customer base if applicable. Identify common characteristics, preferences, behaviors, and purchasing patterns among your current customers. This information can provide valuable insights into your target audience.

5. **Identify Pain Points and Needs:** Understand the pain points, challenges, and needs of your target audience within your niche. Determine how your products, services, or content can address these pain points and provide solutions.

6. **Consider User Intent:** Consider the intent behind users' interactions with your website. Determine whether visitors are seeking information, looking to make a purchase, seeking entertainment, or engaging with your content for other reasons. Tailor your website's content and features to align with user intent.

7. **Evaluate Keywords and Search Trends:** Analyze relevant keywords and search trends related to your industry and niche. Use tools like Google Keyword Planner, SEMrush, or Ahrefs to identify popular search terms and topics within your target audience's interests.

8. **Monitor Social Media Engagement:** Monitor social media platforms to observe conversations, trends, and discussions relevant to your industry. Pay attention to engagement metrics, comments, and interactions with content related to your niche.

9. **Test and Iterate:** Continuously test and iterate your website's content, features, and marketing strategies based on user feedback and analytics data. Use A/B

testing, heatmaps, and user behavior analysis tools to optimize user experiences and conversions.

10. **Stay Flexible:** Keep your target audience profiles flexible and adaptable to changes in market dynamics, consumer preferences, and industry trends. Regularly revisit and update your audience personas to ensure they remain relevant and accurate.

If you follow these steps and invest time in understanding your target audience, you can create a website that effectively engages and resonates with your intended users, ultimately driving success and achieving your business objectives.

Conducting Audience Research, know what your users want

Conducting audience research is a fundamental aspect of building a successful website. Your website exists to serve your audience, whether they're potential customers, clients, or simply visitors seeking information or entertainment. By gaining insights into their preferences, needs, and behaviors, you can tailor your website to meet their expectations and drive engagement. In this section, we'll explore various methods for conducting audience research and how to leverage the insights gained to optimize your website.

Understanding your audience is crucial for several reasons. By knowing what topics, formats, and styles resonate with your audience, you can create content that is more likely to capture their interest and keep them engaged. Audience research helps you identify pain points, preferences, and expectations, allowing you to optimize your website's design, navigation, and functionality to provide a seamless and improved user experience.

Understanding your audience also empowers you to customize your marketing messages, channels, and strategies for more targeted reach and enhanced conversion rates. Through comprehensive audience research, you can uncover valuable insights that distinguish you from competitors, enabling you to offer unique value propositions and better address the needs of your target market.

There are numerous methods for conducting audience research, each offering unique advantages and insights. Let's go through the main five effective approaches I've used in the past.

1. **Surveys and Questionnaires:** Surveys allow you to gather structured data from a large number of respondents quickly and efficiently. You can use online survey tools to create custom surveys and distribute them via email, social media, or your website. Be sure to ask a mix of closed-ended and open-ended ques-

tions to gather both quantitative and qualitative insights.

2. **Interviews and Focus Groups:** In-depth interviews and focus groups provide an opportunity for more nuanced and detailed discussions with your target audience. These methods allow you to probe deeper into their thoughts, preferences, and motivations, uncovering valuable insights that may not emerge in surveys alone. Conducting interviews and focus groups can be time-consuming and resource-intensive but can yield rich qualitative data.

3. **Website Analytics:** Analyzing website analytics data provides valuable insights into your audience's behavior, preferences, and demographics. Tools like Google Analytics track metrics such as website traffic, bounce rate, time on page, and conversion rates, allowing you to understand how users interact with your site. By segmenting your audience based on factors like age, gender, location, and interests, you can gain a better understanding of who your visitors are and what they're looking for.

4. **Social Media Monitoring:** Social media platforms are rich sources of audience insights, with users often sharing their thoughts, opinions, and preferences publicly. By monitoring social media conversations related to your industry, brand, or products, you can uncover trends, sentiment, and common pain points among your audience. Social listening tools like Hootsuite, Sprout Social, and Brand watch can help

you track mentions, hashtags, and keywords across multiple social media platforms.

5. **Competitor Analysis:** Analyzing your competitors' websites, content, and marketing strategies can provide valuable benchmarking data and insights into what resonates with your shared audience. Look for gaps, opportunities, and areas where you can differentiate yourself by offering unique value propositions or addressing unmet needs.

Once you've gathered audience insights through various research methods, it's essential to translate those findings into actionable improvements for your website.

Use audience research to inform your content strategy, including topic selection, content formats, tone of voice, and messaging. Create content that addresses your audience's interests, pain points, and frequently asked questions, positioning your website as a valuable resource in your niche.

Also apply audience insights to optimize your website's user experience, including navigation, layout, and functionality. Without forgetting the use of heatmaps, user testing, and feedback tools to identify areas for improvement and make data-driven decisions to enhance usability and engagement.

By now, you recognize the importance of tailoring your website's content, offers, and recommendations to align with user preferences, behaviors, and demographics. Therefore, incorporating personalization features like dynamic content blocks, recommended products, and personalized messaging is a strategic move to enhance the relevance and individualized experience for every visitor.

Use this audience data to inform your SEO and keyword strategy, identifying the topics, keywords, and search queries your audience is most interested in. Optimize your website's content, meta tags, and internal linking structure to improve visibility and attract organic traffic from search engines.

Additionally apply audience insights to optimize your website's conversion funnel, identifying barriers to conversion and opportunities for improvement. Test different calls-to-action, landing page designs, and checkout processes to maximize conversions and drive revenue.

Conducting audience research is a continuous process that requires ongoing effort and attention. Whether you're launching a new website or optimizing an existing one, investing in audience research is essential for long-term success.

Crafting User Personas

User personas are fictional representations of your target audience segments, based on real data and insights gathered through audience research. Crafting user personas allows you to empathize with your audience, understand their goals, motivations, and pain points, and tailor your website to meet their specific needs.

Let's explore the process of creating user personas and how they can inform your website design, content strategy, and marketing efforts.

Assuming you have gathered insights about your audience through various research methods, as discussed in the previous section. Analyze data from surveys, interviews, website analytics, social media monitoring, and competitor analysis to identify common patterns, preferences, and behaviors among your target audience segments.

Once you have collected sufficient data, group your audience into distinct segments based on factors such as demographics, psychographics, behavior, and other needs to make it easy to identify your audience segments. Common segmentation criteria include age, gender, location, income level, job role, interests, preferences, and pain points. Each segment represents a unique subset of your audience with specific characteristics and needs.

With your audience segments identified, you can begin crafting user personas that represent each segment in detail. User personas typically include the following components:

- **Name:** Give each persona a descriptive name to humanize them and make them more relatable.
- **Demographics:** Include details such as age, gender, location, marital status, education level, and occupation.
- **Background:** Provide information about their personal and professional background, including their goals, challenges, interests, and values.
- **Goals and Motivations:** Identify the primary goals, aspirations, and motivations that drive each persona's behavior and decision-making.
- **Pain Points and Challenges:** Outline the common obstacles, frustrations, and challenges that each persona faces in achieving their goals.
- **Behavior and Preferences:** Describe how each persona behaves online, their preferred channels, devices, and content consumption habits.
- **Quotes and Insights:** Include direct quotes or insights gathered from interviews or surveys to capture the persona's voice and perspective.

To make user personas more impactful, consider adding visual elements such as photos or illustrations to represent each persona visually. This helps stakeholders visualize and empathize with the personas, fostering a deeper understanding of their needs and preferences. Additionally, consider creating narrative scenarios or user stories that illustrate how each persona interacts with your website and the challenges they encounter along the way.

Once you have created user personas, use them as a reference point to inform various aspects of your website design, content strategy, and marketing efforts. For example:

- **Website Design:** Tailor your website's layout, navigation, and functionality to align with the preferences and behaviors of your target personas. Consider how each persona would interact with your site and prioritize features and content that meet their specific needs.
- **Content Strategy:** Develop content that resonates with your personas, addressing their goals, interests, and pain points. Use the language, tone, and messaging that appeals to each persona and provides value to their unique needs.
- **Marketing and Messaging:** Customize your marketing messages, channels, and campaigns to target each persona effectively. Craft personalized campaigns that speak directly to the motivations and aspirations of your personas, increasing engagement and conversions.

Crafting user personas is a valuable exercise that helps you understand your audience on a personal level and tailor your website to meet their specific needs. By empathizing with your personas and aligning your website design, content strategy, and marketing efforts accordingly, you can create a more engaging and relevant experience for your target audience, driving success and satisfaction for both users and your business.

Tailoring Design and Content to Your Audience

Once you've crafted detailed user personas and gained a deep understanding of your audience, the next step is to tailor your website's design and content to meet their specific needs, a user centric experience, preferences, and expectations. In this section, we'll explore the strategies I use for creating a user-centric experience by aligning your website's design and content with the characteristics and goals of your target audience.

User experience (UX) design focuses on creating intuitive, efficient, and enjoyable interactions between users and your website. Consider the following principles when designing your website's UX:

- **Simplicity:** Keep your website design clean, clutter-free, and easy to navigate. Avoid overwhelming users

with excessive visuals or complicated layouts.
- **Accessibility:** Ensure that your website is accessible to users of all abilities, including those with disabilities. Provide alternative text for images, use descriptive headings and labels, and design with color contrast in mind.
- **Mobile Responsiveness:** As the prevalence of mobile browsing continues to soar, ensuring mobile responsiveness is paramount in your website design. Tailor your site's layout and features to seamlessly adapt to diverse screen sizes and resolutions. However, it's essential to acknowledge that this may not apply universally. Stay vigilant with your analytics to discern which devices users are utilizing to access your site and develop to tailored to your specific needs.
- **Consistency:** Maintain consistency across your website in terms of design elements, navigation menus, and branding. Use familiar patterns and conventions to make it easy for users to navigate and understand your website.

In addition to your website's UX, personalization involves delivering tailored content and experiences to individual users based on their preferences, behavior, and demographic information. Leverage user data and segmentation to personalize the following aspects of your website's content:

- **Recommendations:** Recommend relevant products, services, or content based on users' past behavior, interests, or preferences. Use algorithms to suggest related items or content that users are likely to find valuable.
- **Dynamic Content:** Display dynamic content blocks that adapt based on the user's location, browsing history, or stage in the customer journey. For example, show different messaging to first-time visitors versus returning customers.
- **Customized Messaging:** Craft personalized messages and calls-to-action (CTAs) that resonate with each user persona. Use language, tone, and imagery that speaks directly to their goals, motivations, and pain points.

Incorporate user feedback to refine your website's design and content to better meet the needs of your audience. Encourage users to provide feedback through surveys, polls, feedback forms, or interactive elements on your website. Use this feedback to identify areas for improvement and make iterative changes to enhance the user experience.

You can always A/B test and optimize accordingly. A/B testing involves comparing two versions of a web page or element to determine which performs better in terms of user engagement, conversions, or other key metrics. Use A/B testing to experiment with different design elements, layouts, or content variations and measure the impact on user behavior. Continuously optimize your website based on the insights gained from A/B testing to maximize its effectiveness.

Tailoring your website's design and content to your audience is essential for creating a user-centric experience that resonates with your target users. By understanding their preferences, behaviors, and needs through detailed user personas, you can design a website that meets their expectations, drives engagement, and ultimately leads to greater satisfaction and success for both users and your business.

Depending on your business niche your personalization strategy can vary in many ways so always keep an open mind about it.

CHAPTER 4 - CONTENT STRATEGY

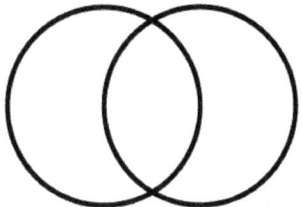

Crafting an effective content strategy is paramount in today's digital landscape, were relevance and engagement reign supreme. In this exploration of content strategy, we delve into the journey of Emily, a digital entrepreneur navigating the complexities of online visibility and content creation. Through her experiences, we'll uncover critical components of content creation. Join us as we unravel the story of Emily and glean insights into the art and science of content strategy.

A Tale of Protection and Compliance

In the world of online content creation, there lived a diligent content creator named Emily. Emily was passionate about crafting engaging well written articles that resonate with her audience. She always checked for spelling and grammar, created captivating videos, and stunning visuals to share with her users. However, amidst her creative endeavors, Emily understood the importance of safeguarding her intellectual property and navigating the complexities of copyright law.

As Emily embarked on her content creation journey, she delved into the realm of copyright basics. With a keen eye for detail, she learned that the moment her ideas took form whether through written prose or digital imagery, they were imbued with the protective cloak of copyright. Armed with this knowledge, Emily felt empowered to assert her ownership rights over her original works.

Yet, Emily also recognized the value of collaboration and distribution, as well as the need to respect the creative rights of others. When sourcing third-party content for her projects, she treaded cautiously, ensuring that she obtained the proper licenses and permissions. Through royalty-free stock media platforms and Creative Commons repositories, Emily discovered a treasure trove of resources that enriched her content without infringing on the rights of others.

In her quest to protect her own creations, Emily adorned her digital assets with copyright notices, signaling to the world that her works were not to be trifled with. She established clear terms of use and licensing agreements, forging a shield against unauthorized reproduction or distribution. With the aid of digital rights management tools,

Emily fortified her content against would-be pirates, deterring illicit copying or alteration.

Despite her vigilance, Emily remained vigilant, keeping a watchful eye on the vast expanse of the digital landscape. Through diligent monitoring and enforcement efforts, she swiftly addressed any instances of infringement, wielding the sword of justice to defend her content kingdom. With each takedown notice sent and legal remedy pursued, Emily stood firm in her commitment to upholding the integrity of her creations.

Through her journey, Emily understood that the path to content copyright compliance was ever-evolving. She remained steadfast in her pursuit of knowledge, staying informed about legal developments and seeking counsel from seasoned legal experts. With each challenge overcome and lesson learned, Emily emerged stronger, her content fortress fortified against the storms of uncertainty.

Emily's dedication to protecting her content copyrights and navigating legalities paid off handsomely. Her audience trusted her as a beacon of integrity in the digital realm, drawn to the authenticity and quality of her creations. With her content kingdom secure and her creative spirit unbound, Emily continued to inspire and captivate audiences far and wide, leaving an indelible mark on the vast canvas of the internet.

Crafting Compelling Call-to-Actions (CTAs)

Countless voices clamor for attention online, there exists a powerful tool capable of guiding users towards desired actions: the Call-to-Action (CTA). Emily, who is a seasoned content creator understands the importance of crafting compelling CTAs to engage and motivate her audience.

As Emily embarked on her content creation journey, she realized that a well-crafted CTA could be the difference between passive viewers and active participants. With this insight, Emily set out to master the art of persuasion through strategic messaging and enticing prompts.

Emily began her quest by delving into the psychology behind effective CTAs. She understood that humans are inherently driven by the desire for gratification and the fear of missing out. Armed with this knowledge, Emily tailored her CTAs to appeal to her audience's emotions and aspirations, leveraging the power of anticipation and urgency.

Emily knew that clarity and simplicity were paramount when crafting CTAs. She avoided ambiguity and jargon, opting instead for concise and action-oriented language that left no room for confusion. Whether it was "Sign Up Now" or "Shop the Sale," Emily's CTAs left no doubt about the desired action.

To entice her audience further, Emily made sure to highlight the benefits of taking action. Whether it was the promise of exclusive discounts, valuable insights, or free resources, Emily's CTAs emphasized the value proposition, compelling users to act in their own best interest.

One of Emily's most potent tactics was instilling a sense of urgency in her CTAs. By employing phrases like "Limited Time Offer" or "Act Now," Emily encouraged her audience to seize the moment, knowing that procrastination could mean missing out on a valuable opportunity.

Emily understood that not all CTAs were created equal. She tailored her calls-to-action to align with the user's journey, whether they were at the awareness, consideration, or decision stage. By offering relevant CTAs at each touchpoint, Emily ensured a seamless and intuitive user experience.

But Emily's journey didn't end with the creation of compelling CTAs. She knew that continuous testing and iteration were essential for optimization. By experimenting with different messaging, designs, and placements, Emily gleaned valuable insights into what resonated most with her audience, refining her CTAs for maximum impact.

Finally, Emily diligently tracked the performance of her CTAs, monitoring metrics like click-through rates, conversion rates, and engagement levels. Armed with this data, Emily could gauge the effectiveness of her CTAs and make informed decisions to further optimize her content strategy.

Emily's mastery of crafting compelling CTAs transformed her content from mere information to irresistible invitations. With each well-placed prompt, Emily guided her audience towards meaningful actions, driving engagement, conversions, and ultimately, success.

Lead Generation Strategies

As Emily continues her journey navigating through the digital landscape, she eventually became, a savvy digital marketer who understands that the lifeblood of any business lies in its ability to generate leads. She now employs a diverse array of strategies to captivate her audience and cultivate valuable relationships.

At the heart of Emily's approach to lead generation lies a deep understanding of its essence. She recognizes that lead generation is not merely about amassing contacts but about fostering genuine connections with individuals who have expressed interest in her brand or offerings.

Emily begins her lead generation journey by creating compelling content offers designed to attract and engage her target audience. Whether it's an insightful e-book, an informative webinar, or an exclusive discount, Emily's content provides tangible value to her prospects, enticing them to take the next step.

To enhance the performance of her content offers, Emily diligently optimizes her landing pages for conversion. She ensures that each landing page is visually captivating, straightforward to navigate, and furnished with compelling CTAs. By eliminating distractions such as excessive pop-ups or irrelevant links and guiding visitors towards the desired action, such as downloading a free e-book or signing up for a newsletter, Emily significantly boosts the chances of lead capture.

Moreover, Emily recognizes the immense potential of social media platforms, she leverages them as powerful tools for lead generation and regularly shares her content offers across various social channels, engaging her audience and encouraging them to interact, share, and ultimately, become leads.

Email marketing remains a cornerstone of Emily's lead generation strategy. Armed with a robust email list acquired through her content offers, Emily crafts personalized and relevant email campaigns tailored to the needs and interests of her subscribers. By delivering valuable content directly to their inboxes, Emily nurtures her leads and guides them through the sales funnel. She understands the allure of exclusive promotions and incentives in driving lead generation. Whether it's a limited-time discount, a special giveaway, or a VIP access pass, Emily uses these incentives to entice prospects to take action and provide their contact information.

To further expand her reach and credibility, Emily actively engages in thought leadership activities and guest posting opportunities. By sharing her expertise and insights on industry-related topics, Emily establishes herself as a trusted authority within her niche, attracting qualified leads who resonate with her message.

Throughout her lead generation efforts, Emily remains vigilant in analyzing data and iterating her strategies based on insights gleaned from metrics and analytics. By monitoring key performance indicators such as conversion rates, lead quality, and customer acquisition cost, Emily continuously refines her approach to achieve optimal results.

Ultimately, Emily's lead generation strategies are not just about acquiring leads but about nurturing relationships and driving sustainable growth for her business. By delivering value, fostering engagement, and prioritizing the needs of her audience, Emily lays the foundation for long-term success.

Maintaining a Unique and Engaging Content Strategy

As Emily's journey continues to unfold, she understands the importance of maintaining a unique and engaging content strategy to keep her audience captivated and her brand top-of-mind. In this final section of our chapter, we delve into Emily's approach to sustaining momentum and fostering ongoing engagement through her content strategy.

Emily's content strategy requires a constant commitment to creativity and innovation. She understands that in a crowded digital landscape, standing out requires daring to be different. She continually pushes the boundaries of conventional marketing norms, experimenting with new formats, storytelling techniques, and interactive elements to capture her audience's imagination.

While Emily embraces innovation, she also recognizes the importance of staying true to her brand's values and voice. Consistency in messaging and tone reinforces brand identity and fosters trust and familiarity among her audience. Emily's content reflects her brand's unique personality, resonating authentically with her target demographic, while she remains attuned to evolving trends and preferences. Emily also continues to monitor shifts in consumer behavior, emerging technologies, and platform algorithms, adjusting her content strategy accordingly. By staying ahead of the curve, Emily ensures that her content remains relevant and impactful in an ever-changing landscape. She understands that successful content strategies go beyond mere dissemination of information, they foster community and conversation. She actively engages with her audience across various channels, responding to comments, soliciting feedback, and facilitating discussions around her content. By nurturing a sense of belonging and inclusivity, Emily cultivates a loyal and engaged community around her brand.

As with all aspects of her marketing efforts, Emily approaches her content strategy with a mindset of continuous improvement. She routinely evaluates the performance of her content, leveraging analytics and feedback to identify areas for enhancement. Whether it's refining messaging, optimizing distribution channels, or experimenting with new formats, Emily is committed to refining her content strategy to achieve greater impact and resonance. Recognizing the continual need for content improvement, Emily collaborates with a team of colleagues located abroad and occasionally delegates content creation tasks to them.

Amidst the ongoing hustle and bustle of digital marketing, Emily takes the time to celebrate milestones and achievements along the way. Whether it's reaching a significant follower milestone, garnering widespread recognition for a standout piece of content, or achieving a notable uptick in engagement, Emily acknowledges and appreciates the successes that fuel her motivation and drive.

As Emily concludes another chapter in her digital marketing journey, she remains steadfast in her commitment to maintaining a unique and engaging content strategy. By embracing creativity, staying true to her brand, adapting to change, fostering community, and continuously striving for improvement, Emily sets the stage for sustained growth and impact in the dynamic world of digital marketing.

With each piece of content she creates, Emily leaves a lasting impression on her audience, forging successful and meaningful connections that endure beyond the digital realm.

"Remember, whether it's through storytelling like in this chapter or other means, the power of content lies in its ability to connect, engage, and inspire."

CHAPTER 5 - DESIGN AND USER EXPERIENCE

Principles of User-Centric Design

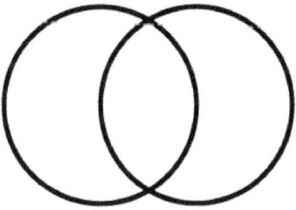

When it comes to designing a website, prioritizing the user experience is very important. User-centric design, also known as user-centered design (UCD), is an approach that focuses on understanding the needs, preferences, and behaviors of users throughout the design process. By placing the user at the center of decision-making, designers can create websites that are intuitive, engaging, and ultimately more successful. As we explained in previous chapters, let's review these next 8 principles of UCD.

1. **User Research:** The foundation of user-centric design lies in thorough user research. This involves

gathering insights into the target audience's demographics, preferences, behaviors, and pain points. Through techniques such as surveys, interviews, and usability testing, designers can gain a deep understanding of user needs.

2. **Define User Personas:** Once user research is complete, designers create user personas, fictional characters that represent different segments of the target audience. These personas help designers empathize with users and make informed design decisions that align with their needs and goals.

3. **Focus on Usability:** Usability is a core principle of user-centric design. Websites should be easy to use, intuitive, and efficient. Designers should prioritize clear navigation, logical information architecture, and intuitive user interfaces to ensure a seamless browsing experience.

4. **Content Strategy:** Effective content is essential for engaging users and meeting their needs. User-centric design involves crafting content that is relevant, informative, and easy to digest. Designers should consider the user's context and tailor content to address their questions and concerns.

5. **Accessibility:** Accessibility is a key aspect of user-centric design, ensuring that websites are usable by people of all abilities. Designers should adhere to web

accessibility standards, such as providing alternative text for images, using semantic HTML markup, and ensuring keyboard navigation.

6. **Iterative Design Process:** User-centric design is iterative, meaning that it involves continuous feedback and refinement. Designers create prototypes and gather feedback from users through usability testing, incorporating insights to improve the design iteratively.

7. **Mobile Responsiveness:** With the increasing use of mobile devices, designing for mobile responsiveness is crucial. User-centric design involves optimizing websites for various screen sizes and devices, ensuring a consistent and seamless experience across platforms.

8. **Empathy and Human-Centered Approach:** At its core, user-centric design is about empathy, understanding the user's perspective, and designing solutions that address their needs and pain points. By adopting a human-centered approach, designers can create meaningful and impactful experiences for users.

In essence, user-centric design is about putting the needs and preferences of users first. By embracing principles such as user research, usability, accessibility, and empathy, designers can create websites that resonate with users and drive positive outcomes.

Optimizing Website Navigation

Imagine walking through a bustling city, trying to find your way without any signs or directions. Frustrating, right? That's how it feels for users navigating a poorly designed website. Among all the websites I have built over the years I've been able to summarize a series of key points to optimize website navigation. Let's uncover the ten key points that define effective website navigation.

- **1. Clear Hierarchy and Organization:** Picture this: organizing a cluttered room into neatly labeled drawers and shelves. Similarly, you can structure your website content with a clear hierarchy, ensuring that users could easily find what they needed without rummaging through digital clutter.
- **2. Consistent Navigation Menus:** Just like the reliable landmarks that guide us through familiar streets, always maintain consistent navigation menus across your website. No matter where users venture into, they can always rely on the comforting familiarity of the navigation bar in the same spot.
- **3. Descriptive Labels:** Think of navigation labels as signposts on a hiking trail – clear, concise, and pointing in the right direction. Choose descriptive labels

that accurately reflect the content of each page, ensuring users know exactly where they are heading.

- **4. Visual Cues:** Imagine following a trail of breadcrumbs through a dense forest – visual cues serve a similar purpose in website navigation. Incorporate subtle hints like icons and color changes to guide users' attention and highlight interactive elements along the way.
- **5. Search Functionality:** Just like having a trusty map in your backpack, implement a search function to help users navigate swiftly, especially in a vast digital landscape. With a simple search box, users can find what they need in seconds, no matter how deep they go into.
- **6. Breadcrumbs:** Ever followed a trail of breadcrumbs back home? Breadcrumbs on websites serve as a similar purpose, offering users a clear path to navigate backward through the site's hierarchy. No more feeling lost in the digital wilderness!
- **7. Responsive Design:** In today's mobile-centric world, optimizing navigation for smaller screens is important. Embrace responsive design techniques, ensuring that your website's navigation remains sleek and intuitive, whether viewed on a desktop or a smartphone.
- **8. User Testing:** Invite friends to test-drive your newly designed road map. Conduct usability testing to gather feedback from real users, observing how they interact with the navigation system and fine-tun-

ing it based on their insights. Do so over and over until your feedback is well balanced.
- 9. **Accessibility Considerations:** Just like adding ramps for wheelchair access, ensure that your website navigation is accessible to all users, regardless of ability. From keyboard navigation options to descriptive text for screen readers, make accessibility be at the forefront of your design.
- 10. **Performance Optimization:** Imagine trimming excess baggage to lighten your load on a hike – that's how you should optimize your website for performance. By removing unnecessary elements and optimizing loading times, you can ensure users can navigate swiftly without any frustrating delays.

Incorporating these strategies has transformed website navigation into a user-friendly digital landscape, guiding visitors on a seamless journey to their desired destinations on many websites I've build. With clear signposts, intuitive pathways, and responsive guidance, navigating your website can become as effortless as a leisurely stroll through a well-marked trail.

Visual Design and Branding Guidelines

Certainly! Visual design and branding guidelines are essential components in crafting the identity and atmosphere of a website. Let's explore how these elements can be harnessed to craft a captivating online presence.

Imagine walking into a well-designed store with vibrant colors, sleek displays, and a cohesive brand identity. The experience is not only visually appealing but also leaves a lasting impression. Similarly, when users visit a website, they should feel immersed in a visually cohesive environment that reflects the brand's identity and values.

Visual design encompasses various aspects such as color schemes, typography, imagery, and layout. Each element contributes to the overall aesthetic appeal and usability of the website. When designing a website, it's essential to establish clear branding guidelines to ensure consistency across all visual elements.

Small details like color palettes play a significant role in evoking emotions and conveying brand personality. By selecting a primary color palette that aligns with the brand's identity, you can create a cohesive visual experience. For example, a technology company might opt for a modern and sophisticated color scheme, while a children's brand may choose bright and playful colors.

Like colors, typography is another crucial aspect of visual design. The choice of fonts can greatly impact readability and brand perception. Selecting complementary typefaces for headings, body text, and other elements helps maintain consistency and readability across the website.

Imagery also plays a vital role in conveying the brand's message and connecting with the audience on an emotional level. High-quality photos, illustrations, and graphics can enhance the visual appeal of the website and reinforce the brand's narrative. Whether using custom photography or stock images, it's essential to ensure that the visuals align with the brand's identity and resonate with the target audience.

The last important point would be the layout design which involves organizing content in a visually appealing and user-friendly manner. A well-structured layout guides users through the website and highlights key information effectively. By incorporating whitespace, clear navigation menus, and intuitive page structures, you can create a seamless browsing experience for users.

Branding guidelines serve as a roadmap for maintaining visual consistency across all touchpoints. These guidelines typically include specifications for logo usage, color palettes, typography, imagery style, and more. By adhering to these guidelines, you can ensure that every aspect of the website reflects the brand's identity and reinforces its values.

In summary, visual design and branding guidelines are integral to creating a memorable and engaging website. By carefully crafting color schemes, typography, imagery, and layout, you can captivate your audience and leave a lasting impression.

> *"Consistency is key, so be sure to establish clear branding guidelines to maintain visual coherence across all aspects of your website."*

Accessibility Considerations for All Users

Ensuring accessibility for all users is a fundamental aspect of web design, allowing everyone, regardless of ability, to access and interact with the content effectively. Let's explore some key considerations for creating an inclusive online experience.

Imagine navigating a website using only a keyboard or screen reader, unable to see or use a mouse. For individuals with disabilities such as visual impairments, motor disabilities, or cognitive limitations, accessing and navigating websites can present significant challenges. By prioritizing accessibility in web design, we can ensure that everyone can access and use digital content comfortably.

One of the most critical aspects of web accessibility is providing alternative text for images. Screen readers rely on alternative text (alt text) to describe images to users who cannot see them. When adding images to a website, it's essential to include descriptive alt text that conveys the content and purpose of the image. This ensures that individuals using screen readers can understand the context of the images.

Another essential consideration is providing keyboard navigation options. Many users, especially those with motor disabilities, rely on keyboards to navigate websites instead of traditional mice. Designing websites with keyboard accessibility in mind ensures that users can navigate through links, buttons, and interactive elements using only the tab and arrow keys. Additionally, ensuring that keyboard focus is clearly visible helps users understand their current location on the page.

Color contrast is also crucial for users with visual impairments, such as color blindness or low vision. Ensuring sufficient contrast between text and background colors improves readability and usability for all users. Following established accessibility guidelines, such as the Web Content Accessibility Guidelines (WCAG), helps ensure that color choices meet the necessary contrast ratios.

Additionally providing captions and transcripts for multimedia content, such as videos and audio recordings, ensures accessibility for users who are deaf or hard of hearing. Captions provide a text-based representation of spoken content, while transcripts offer a written version of the entire audio or video content. Including these alternatives ensures that all users can access the information presented in multimedia formats.

Form accessibility is another critical consideration in web design. Providing clear labels, error messages, and instructions helps users understand form fields and complete tasks successfully. On top of that, ensuring that form fields are properly labeled and accessible via keyboard navigation ensures usability for all users.

By considering factors such as responsive design, which ensures accessibility across various devices and screen sizes, you can guarantee that content remains usable on smartphones, tablets, and desktop computers alike. Accessibility in web design is crucial for fostering inclusive digital experiences. By integrating features that cater to diverse user needs, including those with disabilities, your website becomes accessible to all. Embracing accessibility principles not only enhances usability but also promotes inclusivity, fostering a more equitable online environment for everyone.

CHAPTER 6 - WEBSITE OPTIMIZATION

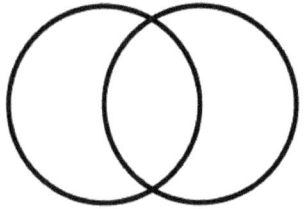

As we embark on the journey of website optimization, I'm reminded of the countless hours spent refining and perfecting my online platform. From the early days of crafting my website's design to the ongoing process of fine-tuning its performance, every step has been a lesson in the art of optimization. Through trial and error, I've discovered the transformative power of strategic tweaks and enhancements, each aimed at elevating the user experience and maximizing results.

In this chapter, together, we'll delve into the intricacies of fine-tuning every aspect of your online presence, from design elements to performance metrics. I'll provide you with practical strategies and actionable tips to help you unlock the full potential of your website.

Whether you're a seasoned webmaster seeking to enhance your existing platform or a newcomer looking to build from scratch, this chapter will equip you with the tools and knowledge needed to optimize your website for success.

Personalizing Online Experience

As someone deeply invested in providing personalized online experiences, I've discovered the incredible impact it can have on user engagement and conversion rates. Let me share with you the strategies my team and I have employed to personalize the online experience on my website.

Firstly, we start by getting to know our audience through user profiling and segmentation like I've mentioned in earlier chapters. By gathering data on their demographics, browsing habits, and preferences, we can divide them into distinct groups. This enables us to tailor our content and recommendations to better suit their needs and interests.

Once we've segmented our audience, we leverage dynamic content customization to deliver personalized experiences. Using advanced content management systems, we serve up relevant content based on factors like their past interactions, location, or interests. This ensures that each visitor receives content that speaks directly to them.

We also pay close attention to user behavior through behavioral targeting. By analyzing metrics such as clicks, page views, and time spent on site, we gain insights into individual preferences. This allows us to fine-tune our recommendations and tailor the online experience to each user's unique preferences.

In addition, we use contextual messaging and notifications to deliver timely and relevant messages. Whether it's a personalized push notification or an email reminder about an upcoming event, we make sure our communications are tailored to the user's current context.

Furthermore, we give users control over their experience through preference management. By allowing them to customize their content preferences and privacy settings, we empower them to shape their own online journey.

Through continuous A/B testing and optimization, we refine our personalization strategies to ensure they remain effective and relevant. This iterative process helps us stay ahead of the curve and deliver the best possible experience to our users.

And of course, we prioritize data privacy and compliance every step of the way. By adhering to regulations and best practices, we ensure that user data is handled responsibly and transparently.

In the end, personalization allows us to forge deeper connections with our audience and drive long-term loyalty. By tailoring the online experience to each user's needs and preferences, we create a journey that feels uniquely theirs.

Ensuring Cross-Browser Compatibility

As a web developer, ensuring cross-browser compatibility has always been a top priority for me. When I first started developing websites, I focused primarily on creating designs that looked great on my preferred browser, which was usually Chrome. However, I quickly learned that not all users accessed the web through the same browser. Some preferred Firefox, others Safari, and there were still those loyal to Internet Explorer or Edge.

I realized that if I wanted my websites to reach a wider audience and provide a positive user experience for all visitors, I needed to ensure cross-browser compatibility. This meant testing my websites on multiple browsers and devices to identify any compatibility issues and address them proactively.

I began by familiarizing myself with modern web standards and best practices, such as HTML5, CSS3, and JavaScript frameworks like React and Angular. These technologies provided a solid foundation for building cross-compatible websites that leveraged the latest features and capabilities of modern browsers.

Next, I adopted a responsive web design approach, using media queries and flexible layout techniques to ensure that my websites adapted seamlessly to different screen sizes and resolutions. This allowed users to access my websites on desktops, laptops, tablets, and smartphones without any loss of functionality or usability.

I also embraced the concept of progressive enhancement, building core functionality that worked across all browsers and devices and then layering on additional features and enhancements for modern browsers. This approach ensured that my websites remained functional and accessible even in older or less-capable browsers.

To streamline the testing process and identify compatibility issues more efficiently, I started using cross-browser testing tools and services like BrowserStack and CrossBrowserTesting. These tools allowed me to test my websites on multiple browsers and devices simultaneously, providing real-time feedback on compatibility issues that needed to be addressed.

I made sure to stay informed about browser updates and changes in web standards, regularly updating my websites to address any compatibility issues or security vulnerabilities that arose. I monitored browser usage statistics and user feedback to identify emerging trends and prioritize updates accordingly.

By checking cross-browser compatibility and adopting a proactive approach to testing and optimization, I was able to ensure that my websites delivered a consistent and high-quality user experience across all platforms, browsers, and devices. This not only minimized user frustration but also maximized reach and engagement, ultimately driving conversions and success for my clients and myself.

Implementing Interactive Features and Chatbots

I've always been fascinated by the potential of interactive features to create more dynamic and engaging user experiences. From simple animations and hover effects to more complex interactive elements like sliders, carousels, and interactive forms, I've experimented with a wide range of techniques to bring websites to life and make them more interactive.

One of the most effective ways I've found to engage users and provide personalized assistance is through the use of chatbots. These pre-programmed bots or AI-powered virtual assistants can help users navigate websites, answer common questions, provide product recommendations, and even facilitate transactions.

Online Magic

When implementing chatbots, I start by identifying the most common user inquiries and tasks, such as product inquiries, order tracking, and support requests. I then design a conversational flow that guides users through these tasks and provides helpful responses in real-time.

To create chatbots, I've experimented with various platforms and tools, including third-party chatbot frameworks like Dialogflow, Merlin AI, Microsoft Bot Framework, and IBM Watson Assistant, as well as custom-built solutions using JavaScript and Node.js. Each approach has its advantages and limitations, but the goal is always the same: to create a seamless and intuitive user experience that enhances engagement and drives conversions.

In addition to chatbots, I've also integrated other interactive features into websites to encourage user interaction and exploration. For example, I've implemented interactive maps to help users find nearby locations or visualize geographic data, interactive charts and graphs to present complex information in a more engaging format, and interactive quizzes and surveys to gather feedback and insights from users.

One of my favorite interactive features to implement is the "live chat" functionality, which allows users to connect with customer support representatives in real-time. This feature not only provides immediate assistance to users but also helps businesses build stronger relationships with their customers and improve customer satisfaction.

When implementing interactive features, I always prioritize usability and accessibility, ensuring that all users, regardless of their device or abilities, can easily interact with the website and access the information they need. I also regularly monitor user feedback and analytics to identify areas for improvement and refine the interactive features accordingly.

Overall, implementing interactive features and chatbots has been a game-changer for enhancing user engagement, improving customer support, and driving conversions on websites. By embracing the power of interactivity, I've been able to create more dynamic and engaging user experiences that delight users and deliver tangible results for my clients.

Placing Ads Strategically for Monetization

Monetizing my website through strategic ad placement has been an intriguing journey, filled with lessons on balancing revenue generation with maintaining a positive user experience.

First and foremost, finding the right balance between ad revenue and user experience is crucial. While ads can bring in income, bombarding users with intrusive ads can drive them away and tarnish my website's reputation. My aim has always been to seamlessly integrate ads into my website's design, enhancing rather than disrupting the user's browsing experience.

One effective strategy I've found is strategically placing ads within the natural flow of my content. Integrating ads between paragraphs or sections allows me to capture users' attention without interrupting their reading experience. This approach ensures that ads complement the content, increasing the likelihood of user engagement.

Considering the importance of the "above the fold" area – the portion of the webpage visible without scrolling – I've carefully placed high-impact ads in this prime real estate. However, I'm mindful not to overwhelm users with too many ads, as it can negatively impact their experience.

In addition to static display ads, I've explored other ad formats like native ads, interstitial ads, sponsored content, and affiliate marketing links. Native ads seamlessly blend with the surrounding content, making them less intrusive and more engaging. Interstitial ads are good because they usually open in new windows but some don't and can be very invasive. Sponsored content allows brands to promote their products in an organic and relevant manner.

Responsive ad design has also been a priority for me to ensure optimal viewing experiences across different devices and screen sizes. Responsive ads adapt to the user's device, providing a consistent and visually appealing experience regardless of the platform.

Testing and optimization have played a crucial role in refining my ad placement strategy. Conducting A/B tests helps me compare different placements, sizes, and formats to determine what works best for my audience. Analyzing metrics like click-through rates and conversion rates guides me in identifying the most effective ad placements.

Lastly, I value user feedback and monitor user behavior to understand the impact of ad placements on the overall user experience. Soliciting feedback from my audience and tracking user engagement with analytics tools help me continuously refine my ad placement strategy based on data-driven insights.

By striking the right balance between monetization and user experience and continuously refining my ad placement strategy, I've been able to maximize revenue while ensuring a positive browsing experience for my website visitors.

CHAPTER 7 - WEBSITE MAINTENANCE AND SECURITY

Establishing Regular Update Procedures

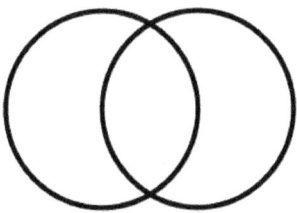

Updating your website is a really important part of the relationship, if you can't do so every day try doing it every week, every two weeks or at least once a month keeping your website up to date will help you in search engines and in their results, we will talk more about that in chapter 9.

" Like communication is the base for a good relationship, updating your website is the base and one of the key elements of the online magic."

Maintaining a website is akin to nurturing a valuable relationship – it requires regular attention and care to ensure its health and vitality. Just as consistent communication forms the foundation of any strong relationship, establishing regular update procedures for your website serves as a cornerstone for its success in the online magic.

Updating your website frequently is important for several reasons. Not only does it demonstrate to visitors that your platform is active and dynamic, but it also plays a crucial role in improving search engine visibility and rankings. Search engines favor fresh, relevant content, and regularly updating your website ensures that it remains relevant and competitive in search results.

While daily updates may not always be feasible, try and make it a priority to update your website at least once a week, if not more frequently. However, even updating every two weeks or on a monthly basis can significantly contribute to the overall health and performance.

For me, implementing a regular update schedule has become ingrained in my workflow, akin to a routine check-up for my online presence. Whether it involves adding new content, refreshing existing pages, optimizing meta tags and descriptions, or installing security updates each update contributes to the growth and vitality of my website.

Establishing regular update procedures will allow you to stay connected with your audience and provide them with fresh and engaging content on a consistent basis. By keeping your website up to date, you'll be able to effectively communicate with your visitors, address their needs and interests, and foster stronger connections with them over time.

Updating a website is not just a task – it's a fundamental aspect of nurturing your online presence and ensuring its long-term success. Just as in any relationship, regular attention and effort are essential for maintaining a strong and vibrant connection with your audience. Through consistent updates and ongoing engagement, you can continue to cultivate a thriving and dynamic online presence that resonates with your audience and delivers value to them.

Utilizing Maintenance Tools and Platforms

In my journey of website maintenance and security, I've come to appreciate the value of utilizing maintenance tools and platforms. These resources have become indispensable assets in my efforts to keep my website running smoothly and securely, allowing me to streamline tasks, identify issues, and implement necessary updates with ease.

Website monitoring software is an indispensable asset in my toolkit for maintaining my online presence. These platforms offer invaluable real-time insights into the performance and uptime of my website, allowing me to stay informed about any issues or downtime that may arise. With timely alerts and notifications, I can quickly address any issues and prevent potential disruptions to the user experience.

To ensure comprehensive monitoring, I utilize both free and paid website monitoring platforms. Free options like UptimeRobot and StatusCake provide basic monitoring capabilities, including uptime checks and performance metrics. Meanwhile, paid platforms such as Pingdom and Site24x7 offer more advanced features such as real-user monitoring, transaction monitoring, and customizable alerts. By leveraging a combination of these tools, I can maintain a proactive approach to website maintenance and deliver a consistently reliable experience to my visitors.

Additionally, content management systems (CMS) play a vital role in simplifying website maintenance tasks. Platforms like WordPress, Joomla, and Drupal provide user-friendly interfaces that allow me to easily update content, add new pages, and manage media files without the need for extensive technical knowledge. With intuitive CMS platforms, I can maintain my website efficiently and focus on delivering valuable content, tools, or services to my audience.

One other the essential maintenance tool I rely on is a website backup solution. Ensuring regular backups of your website is crucial for protecting your data and mitigating the risk of data loss due to unforeseen events such as server failures, hacking attempts, or human error. Many hosting providers offer automated backup solutions as part of their hosting plans, but it's essential to choose your provider carefully to ensure adequate backup coverage.

In addition to hosting-provided backups, there are various free and paid backup solutions available for websites. Free options like UpdraftPlus and BackWPup offer basic backup functionality, allowing you to schedule regular backups and store them locally or in cloud storage services such as Dropbox or Google Drive. For more advanced features and capabilities, paid backup solutions like VaultPress and BackupBuddy provide enhanced security, automatic backups, and one-click restoration options. Regardless of the solution you choose, regularly backing up your website is an essential step in safeguarding your data and ensuring business continuity.

Besides monitoring and backup tools, I've also found immense value in leveraging website optimization platforms to elevate the performance and user experience of my online presence. These comprehensive platforms offer a range of functionalities that delve deep into the intricate details of my website's performance metrics, providing invaluable insights and actionable recommendations for improvement. For instance, Google's PageSpeed Insights is a powerful tool that evaluates the loading speed of my webpages across different devices and provides optimization suggestions to enhance user experience.

Moreover, other website optimization platforms such as GTmetrix, Pingdom, and WebPageTest offer in-depth performance analysis, highlighting areas for improvement in terms of page load times, server response times, and overall website responsiveness. These platforms also assess mobile responsiveness, ensuring that my website delivers a seamless experience across various devices and screen sizes. Additionally, they provide insights into SEO optimization, identifying opportunities to improve search engine visibility and drive organic traffic to my website.

By incorporating insights from these website optimization platforms into my maintenance routine, I can continuously fine-tune my website to deliver optimal performance and user experience. Whether it's optimizing images, minifying CSS and JavaScript files, or implementing caching strategies, these platforms empower me to make informed decisions that positively impact my website's performance and engagement metrics.

Furthermore, in today's digital landscape, security plugins and software play a pivotal role in safeguarding my website against the ever-evolving threat landscape. These essential tools offer a multi-layered defense strategy, encompassing features such as firewall protection, malware scanning, and vulnerability detection to thwart potential cyberattacks.

Among the array of security plugins available, options like Wordfence Security, Sucuri Security, and iThemes Security stand out as popular choices among website owners. These plugins offer comprehensive security functionalities, including real-time threat detection, blacklist monitoring, and file integrity checks, ensuring round-the-clock protection against malicious actors and unauthorized access attempts.

For those seeking more advanced security measures, premium security solutions such as SiteLock and MalCare provide enhanced features like website hardening, automated malware removal, and security audits. While these premium options may require a financial investment, they offer unparalleled peace of mind and robust protection against sophisticated cyber threats.

By integrating security plugins and software into my website maintenance routine, I've been able to proactively defend against security vulnerabilities, mitigate risks, and uphold the trust and integrity of my online presence.

Overall, the utilization of maintenance tools and platforms plays its role in streamlining my website management processes and enhancing its performance, security, and reliability. By leveraging these resources effectively, you can ensure that your website remains healthy, resilient, and optimized for success.

Implementing Security Measures Against Cyber Threats

Implementing robust security measures against cyber threats has become a top priority. With the increasing frequency and sophistication of cyber-attacks, safeguarding my website and protecting sensitive data has become imperative to maintaining trust and credibility with my audience.

Here's how I've approached implementing security measures to fortify my website against potential threats:

1. **Utilizing SSL/TLS Encryption:** One of the foundational security measures I've implemented is SSL/TLS encryption. By encrypting data transmitted between the website and visitors' browsers, you can protect sensitive information such as login credentials, payment details, and personal data from interception by cybercriminals. SSL/TLS certificates not only enhance data security but also inspire trust and confidence among users by displaying the padlock icon and "https://" in the browser address bar.
2. **Implementing Web Application Firewalls (WAF):** Web Application Firewalls serve as a protective bar-

rier between websites and the internet, filtering out malicious traffic and blocking common cyber threats such as SQL injection, cross-site scripting (XSS), and distributed denial-of-service (DDoS) attacks. By deploying a WAF solution, you can proactively detect and mitigate security vulnerabilities in real-time, reducing the risk of website compromise and data breaches.

3. **Regular Security Audits and Vulnerability Scanning:** Conducting regular security audits and vulnerability scanning is essential for identifying and addressing potential weaknesses in any website's infrastructure and codebase. By leveraging automated scanning tools and manual security assessments, you can identify security flaws, misconfigurations, and outdated software that could be exploited by cyber attackers. Addressing these vulnerabilities promptly helps maintain a strong security posture and minimize the risk of exploitation.

4. **Strong Authentication Mechanisms:** Implementing strong authentication mechanisms such as multi-factor authentication (MFA) adds an extra layer of security to any website's login process, reducing the risk of unauthorized access to user accounts. By requiring users to verify their identity through multiple factors such as passwords, biometrics, or one-time codes, this can mitigate the risk of credential theft and unauthorized account access, enhancing overall security.

5. **Regular Software Updates and Patch Management:** Keeping your website's software, plugins, and dependencies up-to-date is crucial for addressing known security vulnerabilities and preventing exploitation by cyber attackers. By regularly installing security patches and updates provided by software vendors and developers, you can close security gaps and ensure that your website's underlying technology remains secure and resilient against emerging threats.
6. **Data Encryption and Secure Storage Practices:** Protecting sensitive data from unauthorized access requires robust encryption and secure storage practices. Always ensure that sensitive information such as user passwords, payment details, and personal data are encrypted both in transit and at rest using industry-standard encryption algorithms. Additionally, adhere to best practices for data storage, limiting access to sensitive data, and implementing strong access controls to prevent unauthorized disclosure or theft.

> *"For payment details is usually best practice to store payment data at your payment provider servers."*

7. **Employee Training and Awareness:** Recognizing that human error can often be a weak link in cybersecurity defenses, try and prioritize employee training and awareness programs to educate staff members about common cyber threats, phishing attacks, and security best practices. By fostering a culture of secu-

rity awareness and vigilance, you can empower employees to recognize and respond effectively to potential security incidents, reducing the likelihood of successful cyber-attacks.

By implementing security measures such as the ones I just mentioned and adopting a proactive approach to cybersecurity, you can mitigate the risk of cyber threats, protect your website and sensitive data, and maintain the trust and confidence of your audience. Constant vigilance, regular assessments, and ongoing improvements are essential for staying ahead of evolving threats and safeguarding your online presence against malicious actors.

Data Protection and Compliance Considerations

Data protection and compliance considerations has become increasingly important in today's digital environment. As data privacy regulations continue to evolve and become more stringent, ensuring compliance with key legislation such as the General Data Protection Regulation (GDPR), California Consumer Privacy Act (CCPA), and other relevant laws has become a top priority for website owners and businesses.

Here's how I've approached data protection and compliance considerations to safeguard sensitive data and ensure regulatory compliance:

1. **Understanding Regulatory Requirements:** The first step in addressing data protection and compliance considerations is to gain a thorough understanding of relevant regulations and legal requirements governing the collection, processing, and storage of personal data. Key regulations such as the GDPR in the European Union and the CCPA in California impose strict obligations on businesses regarding data protection, transparency, and individual rights. By familiarizing with the provisions of these regulations and staying informed about updates and changes, I've been able to ensure compliance with legal requirements and mitigate the risk of regulatory penalties.

2. **Implementing Privacy Policies and Notices:** Transparency and accountability are fundamental principles of data protection regulations, requiring businesses to provide clear and comprehensive privacy policies and notices to users regarding the collection, use, and sharing of their personal information. I've developed and implemented privacy policies that outline my website's data handling practices, including the types of data collected, purposes of processing, data retention periods, and users' rights under applicable regulations. By prominently displaying privacy policies and notices on my website and ensuring they are easily accessible to users, I demonstrate transparency and build trust with my audience.

3. **Obtaining Lawful Basis for Data Processing:** Data protection regulations such as the GDPR require businesses to establish a lawful basis for processing personal data, such as obtaining user consent, fulfilling contractual obligations, or complying with legal obligations. I've implemented mechanisms to obtain explicit consent from users before collecting or processing their personal information, ensuring that data processing activities are lawful, fair, and transparent. By providing users with clear and granular options to consent to specific data processing activities, I respect users' privacy preferences and rights while maintaining compliance with regulatory requirements.
4. **Implementing Data Minimization and Storage Limitation Practices:** Adhering to the principles of data minimization and storage limitation is essential for reducing the risk of unauthorized access, misuse, or retention of personal data beyond what is necessary for the intended purposes. I've implemented practices to collect only the minimum amount of personal data required for specified purposes and to retain data only for as long as necessary to fulfill those purposes or comply with legal requirements. By regularly reviewing and purging outdated or unnecessary data, I minimize the risk of data breaches and ensure compliance with data protection regulations.
5. **Enhancing Data Security Measures:** Protecting personal data from unauthorized access, disclosure, or alteration requires robust data security measures to

safeguard sensitive information against cyber threats and security breaches. I've implemented a multi-layered approach to data security, incorporating encryption, access controls, firewalls, intrusion detection systems, and regular security audits to protect personal data from unauthorized access or misuse. By adopting industry-standard security practices and staying abreast of emerging threats and vulnerabilities, I mitigate the risk of data breaches and ensure the confidentiality, integrity, and availability of personal data.

6. **Facilitating User Rights and Requests:** Data protection regulations grant users various rights regarding their personal data, including the right to access, rectify, erase, restrict processing, and data portability. I've established processes and procedures to facilitate users' exercise of their rights and requests concerning their personal data, ensuring timely responses and compliance with regulatory obligations. By providing clear instructions and mechanisms for users to submit requests and inquiries regarding their personal data, I demonstrate commitment to data protection and accountability.

7. **Monitoring Compliance and Adapting to Regulatory Changes:** Achieving and maintaining compliance with data protection regulations is an ongoing process that requires regular monitoring, assessment, and adaptation to evolving regulatory requirements. I regularly review and update my data protection prac-

tices and policies to ensure alignment with the latest legal developments and industry standards. Additionally, I monitor regulatory enforcement actions, guidance, and best practices to proactively address emerging compliance challenges and mitigate potential risks. By staying vigilant and responsive to regulatory changes, I demonstrate a commitment to data protection and compliance excellence.

In summary, navigating data protection and compliance considerations requires a proactive and comprehensive approach to safeguarding personal data and ensuring regulatory compliance. By understanding legal requirements, implementing robust data protection measures, and fostering a culture of privacy and accountability, you can protect sensitive data, build trust with users, and mitigate the risk of regulatory penalties. Constant vigilance, ongoing assessment, and continuous improvement are essential for maintaining compliance in an ever-changing regulatory landscape.

CHAPTER 8 - MARKETING STRATEGIES

Understanding Internet Marketing Channels

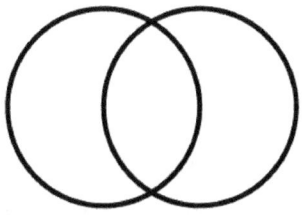

Understanding and using different internet marketing channels is akin to embarking on a thrilling expedition across a vast ocean of possibilities, each promising unique opportunities to connect with my audience and propel my online endeavors forward. Through my journey as a website owner striving to expand my online presence and foster business growth, I've embarked on an exploration of various internet marketing channels and techniques, uncovering their intricacies and leveraging their potential to drive meaningful results.

Through a journey of trials, from submitting websites to search engines to crafting free services and advertising in commercial email newsletters, I've explored a multitude of strategies. What I've gleaned from this experience is that success isn't about focusing on any single tactic but rather integrating a comprehensive approach. By combining these strategies cohesively, business owners like myself can achieve the desired results. It's the synergy of these efforts working together that truly drives success in the digital landscape.

Search Engine Optimization (SEO) serves as the bedrock of my internet marketing strategy, aiming to elevate my website's visibility and ranking in search engine results pages (SERPs). By meticulously optimizing website content, structure, and technical elements according to search engine algorithms, I've bolstered my website's organic search performance, attracting relevant traffic from search giants like Google, Bing, and Yahoo.

SEO combined with relevant interesting content, now called content marketing emerged as a potent force in my quest to engage and resonate with my audience. Through the creation and dissemination of strategic content, ranging from informative articles and guides to captivating videos and infographics, I've positioned my website as a go-to resource tailored to my audience's interests and needs. By consistently delivering high-quality, relevant content across various platforms, including social media and email newsletters, I've expanded my reach and nurtured lasting relationships with my audience.

Social media platforms have become indispensable tools for enhancing brand visibility and fostering meaningful connections with diverse audiences across the digital landscape. By actively cultivating a robust presence on leading platforms such as Facebook, Instagram, Twitter, and LinkedIn, I've been able to nurture authentic engagements, share compelling content derived from my website, and leverage targeted advertising strategies both paid and organic to broaden my brand's exposure and drive traffic back to my website.

Understanding the unique demographics and user behaviors associated with each social media platform has been essential in tailoring my approach to effectively engage with various audience segments. For instance, Facebook boasts a broad user base spanning different age groups, making it an ideal platform for reaching a diverse audience demographic. In contrast, Instagram predominantly appeals to a younger demographic, making it an ideal platform for visually engaging content and influencer collaborations aimed at millennials and Gen Z. Twitter, with its real-time feed and trending topics, offers opportunities for immediate engagement and conversation, while LinkedIn provides a professional networking environment suited for B2B interactions and industry thought leadership.

Moreover, the use of targeted advertising across these platforms allows for precise audience targeting based on demographics, interests, and behaviors, ensuring that promotional efforts are directed towards those most likely to engage with and benefit from the content or offerings presented. By adopting a strategic and diversified approach to social media marketing, I've been able to maximize brand visibility, and foster genuine connections with my audience.

In addition to social media, email marketing still represents an important part of my digital marketing arsenal, providing a direct line of communication to engage with subscribers and nurture relationships over time by driving users back to my social media profiles and finally back to my website. Through strategic email campaigns, personalized content, and meticulous optimization of design and deliverability, I've achieved higher engagement rates and conversions.

Email newsletters are powerful tools for businesses to engage with their audience. However, getting users to sign up for newsletters, whether online or offline, requires thoughtful strategies and effective tactics. Let me share the following tactics I've successfully used in the past for encouraging newsletter sign-ups both in the digital world and the physical world.

Online Strategies:

1. **Compelling Website Pop-Ups:** Implementing eye-catching pop-ups on your website can capture visitors' attention and prompt them to subscribe to your newsletter. Offer incentives such as discounts, free resources, or exclusive content to incentivize sign-ups.

2. **Opt-In Forms on Landing Pages:** Place opt-in forms strategically on your landing pages, ensuring they are prominent and easy to fill out. Clearly communicate the benefits of subscribing to your newsletter and reassure users about privacy and email frequency.

3. **Content Upgrades:** Offer valuable content upgrades, such as ebooks, guides, or templates, in exchange for email sign-ups. Tailor these upgrades to specific blog posts or articles to maximize relevance and appeal to your audience's interests.

4. **Social Media Promotion:** Leverage your social media channels to promote your newsletter and encourage sign-ups. Share sneak peeks of newsletter content, run contests or giveaways exclusive to subscribers, and include sign-up links in your social media stories and posts.

5. **Email Signature Call-to-Action:** Add a call-to-action (CTA) and a sign-up link to your email signature to

capitalize on every communication opportunity. Encourage recipients to subscribe to your newsletter for updates, offers, and valuable content.

Offline Strategies:

1. **In-Store Sign-Up Stations:** Set up sign-up stations in your physical store or at events, trade shows, and conferences. Provide tablets or paper sign-up forms along with clear instructions and incentives to encourage visitors to subscribe to your newsletter.

2. **Business Cards and Flyers:** Include a call-to-action to subscribe to your newsletter on your business cards, flyers, and promotional materials. Offer a QR or a shortened URL for easy access to the sign-up page.

3. **Event Sponsorships and Partnerships:** Partner with local events or organizations and sponsor their activities in exchange for exposure and the opportunity to promote your newsletter. Set up booths or displays with sign-up forms and engage with attendees to encourage subscriptions.

4. **Branded Merchandise Giveaways:** Offer branded merchandise such as pens, stickers, or tote bags at events or as part of promotions. Include information

about your newsletter and a QR code or URL for users to sign up.

5. **Networking and Word-of-Mouth:** Utilize networking opportunities to spread the word about your newsletter. Engage in conversations with customers, partners, and industry contacts, and invite them to subscribe to stay updated on your latest news and offers.

Effective newsletter sign-up strategies require a combination of online and offline tactics to reach and engage with your target audience effectively. By implementing strategies like these, thoughtfully and consistently, businesses can build a robust subscriber base, nurture customer relationships, and drive long-term success with their newsletters. Remember to always send transactional and reminder emails aimed at engaging customers, providing important information, and driving desired actions.

Transactional emails are messages triggered by specific actions or events, such as a purchase confirmation, order status update, password reset, or account registration. These emails are highly relevant and time-sensitive, as they deliver essential information directly related to the user's interaction with a website or application. Transactional emails typically have high open rates because recipients expect and anticipate them. They serve to confirm transactions, provide receipts, and deliver important updates, enhancing the customer experience and instilling trust in the brand.

> *" You can always include a banner or two for product cross-selling purposes in your communications."*

Reminder emails are sent to remind users of important events, deadlines, or actions they need to take. These can include appointment reminders, event invitations, subscription renewals, abandoned cart reminders, or upcoming sales notifications. The goal of reminder emails is to prompt recipients to complete a desired action or engage further with the brand. By sending timely reminders, businesses can increase conversions, reduce churn, and improve customer retention rates. Reminder emails should be personalized, concise, and include clear calls-to-action to encourage recipients to take the desired action promptly.

Collaborating with complementary businesses through email mentions can be another strategic way to expand your reach and tap into new audiences. By exchanging email mentions, you can leverage each other's customer base and credibility to gain exposure and drive traffic to your respective websites or offerings. Whether through joint promotions, co-branded campaigns, or shout-outs in newsletters, partnering with businesses that share a similar target audience can result in mutually beneficial outcomes.

This collaborative approach not only enhances brand visibility but also fosters goodwill and trust among customers.

While email marketing can indeed be cost-effective or even free, there are alternative forms of advertising such as Pay-Per-Click (PPC) advertising, which offer distinct advantages and strategies for reaching target audiences. Whether in the form of text or video, provides a dynamic and versatile means to connect with my intended audience with unparalleled precision and control. Leveraging platforms such as Google Ads and Bing Ads, I've harnessed the potential of PPC campaigns to not only drive traffic but also to enhance conversion rates and optimize return on investment (ROI). This achievement stems from a strategic approach involving meticulous keyword research, ad optimization techniques, and vigilant performance monitoring.

In delving into PPC campaigns, the cornerstone lies in selecting the most pertinent keywords that resonate with my target demographic. Through extensive research and analysis, I identify keywords with high relevance and search volume, ensuring that my ads are displayed to users actively seeking products or services like mine. Furthermore, adept optimization of ad content and structure ensures that my messages are compelling, engaging, and tailored to prompt action from viewers.

The success of PPC campaigns is not merely in their initiation but also in their ongoing management and optimization. Rigorous monitoring of performance metrics, such as click-through rates (CTR), conversion rates, and cost-per-click (CPC), allows for real-time adjustments to maximize efficiency and effectiveness. Through iterative refinement of targeting parameters, ad creatives, and bidding strategies, I continuously fine-tune my PPC campaigns to extract maximum value and deliver optimal results.

In essence, PPC advertising offers a potent toolset for driving targeted traffic, boosting conversions, and optimizing ROI. Through strategic planning, meticulous execution, and ongoing optimization, you can harness the full potential of PPC to propel your online presence and achieve overarching business objectives.

Another effective method to promote your website is through affiliate marketing, which has allowed me to diversify my revenue streams and capitalize on my website's traffic in a highly efficient manner. Through astute collaboration with pertinent affiliate programs, I've unlocked the potential to monetize my online presence with finesse. This symbiotic relationship entails transparently endorsing products or services that align seamlessly with my audience's interests and needs, fostering a sense of trust and credibility among my followers.

The essence of affiliate marketing lies in the cultivation of strategic partnerships that resonate authentically with my brand identity and values. By carefully selecting affiliate programs that offer products or services of genuine value to my audience, I ensure that my promotional efforts remain ethical and impactful. This approach not only cultivates a loyal and engaged audience base but also engenders a sense of integrity and authenticity in my marketing endeavors.

The beauty of affiliate marketing lies in its capacity to generate passive income, allowing me to leverage my website's traffic to drive revenue without the need for active involvement in product development or fulfillment. Through strategic placement of affiliate links, compelling product reviews, and value-driven recommendations, I seamlessly integrate promotional content into my website's ecosystem, enhancing user experience while monetizing organic traffic.

Similar to influencer marketing, affiliate marketing operates on a similar principle. Nowadays, influencer marketing has become increasingly prominent as a dynamic and potent strategy, providing a direct avenue to enhance brand visibility and engagement. Through strategic collaboration with social media influencers and content creators who resonate with my audience, I've harnessed the inherent credibility and influence wielded by these digital tastemakers. Influencer marketing lies in the art of forging authentic and mutually beneficial partnerships with influencers who possess a genuine connection with their followers. By aligning with influencers whose values, interests, and audience demographics align closely with my brand, I've been able to leverage their existing rapport and trust to amplify my message and extend my brand's reach.

One particularly effective tactic within influencer marketing involves harnessing the power of webinars in collaboration with influencers. These live, interactive online events serve as a platform for influencers to share their expertise, insights, and recommendations with their audience in real-time. By co-hosting webinars with influencers relevant to my niche, I've been able to tap into their authority and expertise to deliver value-packed content that resonates deeply with their followers.

Through these collaborative webinars, I've not only expanded my brand's visibility and credibility but also fostered meaningful engagement and trust with a highly targeted audience. By providing valuable insights, actionable advice, and exclusive offers during these webinars, I've cultivated a sense of authenticity and authority around my brand, driving traffic, conversions, and long-term loyalty in the process.

In essence, influencer marketing, coupled with the strategic use of webinars, has proven to be a potent combination for amplifying brand awareness, engagement, and credibility in today's crowded digital landscape.

Grasping the intricacies and synergies among various internet marketing channels has been instrumental in sculpting my digital marketing approach and realizing my online goals. Through the strategic amalgamation of diverse channels such as SEO, content marketing, social media, email, PPC advertising, affiliate marketing, and influencer collaborations, I've not only amplified my online visibility but also bolstered engagement and conversions. This comprehensive strategy has enabled my website to thrive and flourish amidst the dynamic and competitive digital arena.

Moreover, incorporating Facebook apps into my marketing arsenal has further augmented my content distribution and outreach efforts. Leveraging these apps as potent tools for marketing and content dissemination has empowered me to extend my brand's reach, connect with my target audience more effectively, and drive meaningful engagement across various demographics. By tactically integrating Facebook apps into my overarching marketing strategy, I've unlocked new avenues for engagement and interaction, propelling my online presence to new heights.

Creating and Managing a Blog for Content Marketing

Creating and managing a blog for content marketing has been important in my online marketing strategy. Through the art of storytelling, leadership, and value-driven content creation, I've leveraged my blog as a powerful tool for engaging audiences, building brand authority, and driving website traffic. Let me share my experiences and insights on the process of crafting a compelling blog that serves as the cornerstone of my content marketing efforts.

At the heart of every successful blog lies a well-defined content strategy. Before diving into content creation, I took the time to define my target audience, identify their pain points, and understand their content preferences. Armed with this knowledge, I developed a content calendar outlining topics, themes, and publishing schedules aligned with my audience's interests and my business objectives. By focusing on delivering valuable and relevant content that resonates with my audience, I've been able to attract and retain readership while driving organic traffic to my website.

With my content strategy in place, I set out to create blog posts that inform, inspire, and engage my audience. From informative how-to guides and industry insights to compelling storytelling and thought-provoking opinion pieces, I've diversified my content mix to cater to different audience segments and content formats. By prioritizing quality over quantity and maintaining a consistent publishing cadence, I've cultivated a loyal readership and positioned myself as a trusted source of information in my niche. Each blog post serves as an opportunity to showcase my expertise, address customer pain points, and drive engagement through comments, shares, and social interactions.

Never ever forget about search engines, search engine optimization (SEO) plays a crucial role in driving organic traffic to my blog. I've optimized my blog posts for relevant keywords, meta tags, and on-page elements such as images and alt text on images to improve their visibility and ranking in search engine results pages (SERPs). By conducting keyword research, optimizing headlines and meta descriptions, and incorporating internal and external links, I've enhanced the discoverability and accessibility of my blog content. Additionally, I've embraced multimedia content formats such as videos, infographics, and interactive visuals to enhance user experience and improve search engine rankings.

"Alt Text, is short for alternate text, is a descriptive attribute added to the HTML code to provide a textual description of an image on a webpage."

Creating great content is just the first step, promoting it effectively is equally important. I've leveraged a multi-channel approach to promote my blog content across various digital channels, including social media, email newsletters, and online communities. By sharing my blog posts on platforms like Facebook, Twitter, LinkedIn, and Instagram, I've extended my reach and amplified my content's visibility to broader audiences. Additionally, I've nurtured an engaged email subscriber list and leveraged email marketing campaigns to drive traffic to my blog and encourage reader engagement.

Building a thriving blog community requires ongoing engagement and interaction with readers. I've fostered a two-way dialogue with my audience by responding to comments, addressing questions, and soliciting feedback on my blog posts. By actively engaging with readers on social media, participating in online discussions, and hosting live Q&A sessions, I've deepened relationships, built trust, and cultivated a sense of community around my blog. Additionally, I've encouraged user-generated content such as guest posts, reader testimonials, and user-generated reviews to enrich the content ecosystem and foster a sense of ownership among my audience.

Creating and managing a blog for content marketing has been a transformative journey that has allowed me to connect with audiences, showcase my expertise, and drive website traffic through compelling storytelling and valuable content. By establishing a content strategy, crafting compelling content, applying search engine optimization (SEO), promoting across channels, and engaging with readers, I've unlocked the full potential of my blog as a powerful tool for brand building, lead generation, and customer engagement. As I continue to evolve and refine my blogging strategy, I remain committed to delivering high-quality content that informs, inspires, and resonates with my audience, driving sustainable growth and success.

Leveraging Offline Traditional Media for Online Success

Contrary to what some people say or believe, traditional media isn't a relic of the past but a treasure trove waiting to be unlocked. My journey in leveraging traditional media for online success has been nothing short of enlightening. Amidst the allure of digital channels, traditional media including television, radio, newspapers, and magazines still holds significant sway, offering unique opportunities to bolster online presence and drive tangible results.

Embarking on the journey of promoting my website offline was like setting sail into uncharted waters, accustomed to making a living online, this was basically a new world filled with creative opportunities beyond the digital horizon. While the internet offers boundless reach and accessibility, I discovered that offline promotion techniques and integrations provide a tangible and immersive way to connect with audiences in the physical world. Let me take you on a voyage through my experiences and insights on leveraging offline promotion techniques that complemented and enriched my online marketing endeavors.

Networking events and conferences became my ports of call, offering me the chance to expand my professional network, forge meaningful relationships, and reel in leads for my website. As I navigated through industry-specific gatherings, trade shows, and seminars, I seized opportunities to showcase my expertise and engage with potential customers. Whether I was on stage as a speaker, manning an exhibitor booth, or simply mingling with fellow attendees, I made sure to distribute business cards, flyers, and brochures to leave a lasting impression. Following each event, I consistently prioritize post-event communication to nurture potential leads and capitalize on networking opportunities. Whether through personalized email outreach, text messages, or direct calls, I aim to maintain engagement and foster relationships that could lead to sales or referrals. This proactive approach not only demonstrates attentiveness to prospects but also ensures that connections made during the event are effectively leveraged for future business opportunities.

Depending on the type of business, local community engagement is a must to establish a strong presence within the neighborhood. By getting involved in sponsorships, partnerships, and community events, I've showcased my commitment to the local community while connecting with audiences on a local level. Whether it was sponsoring a charity fundraiser, hosting a workshop, or participating in

Online Magic

a neighborhood festival, I used these opportunities to promote my business mission and values.

Television Advertising is a beacon of mass reach and storytelling prowess. Through carefully crafted TV commercials, I've tapped into the captivating power of visual storytelling to showcase my website's offerings to a broad audience. The medium allowed me to build brand recognition, drive traffic, and transcend digital confines. However, while television advertising can be expensive for some businesses, radio advertising proved to be a steadfast companion in reaching targeted audiences with precision and at a much lower cost making my ROI faster. With radio spots, I connected with listeners in their daily routines, sparking engagement and driving traffic through compelling audio storytelling.

Print advertising and direct mail have also proven to be reliable tools in navigating me toward targeted audiences and fostering engagement. Despite the digital age, I've recognized the enduring influence of print media, ranging from newspaper ads and magazine placements to direct mail flyers and postcards. Through compelling ad copy and visually striking designs, I've successfully captured the attention of readers and enticed them to explore my website further.

Additionally, I've integrated guerrilla marketing tactics into my strategy, leveraging unconventional and attention-grabbing methods to promote my business offline. From street art and chalk murals to flash mobs and viral stunts, I've embraced guerrilla marketing as a means to ignite conversations and generate buzz, both online and offline. While these tactics may not suit every business, they are certainly worth considering for their potential impact.

Securing newspaper and magazine features elevated my website's credibility and authority. Editorial coverage provided valuable backlinks, social proof, and brand validation, driving organic traffic and boosting search engine rankings. Public relations and media are always helpful in navigating the tumultuous seas of press coverage and earned media exposure. By crafting compelling press releases and cultivating relationships with journalists and influencers, you can secure valuable media coverage in newspapers, magazines, TV programs, and online publications. Doing so is not only good for exposure, but it also helps your SEO.

As you can see traditional media channels aren't relics of the past but treasures waiting to be discovered, offering opportunities to complement and enrich your online marketing efforts.

> *"Remember, it's all about connecting with your audience, whoever they may be."*

CHAPTER 9 - SEARCH ENGINE OPTIMIZATION (SEO)

Writing SEO-Optimized Content

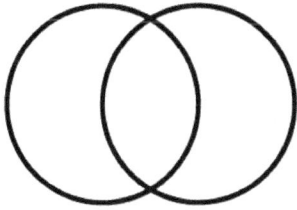

SEO-optimized content has revolutionized digital marketing strategies. Recognizing the significance of keyword research and tailoring content to meet search engine algorithms has empowered businesses and individuals to enhance their website's visibility and draw in organic traffic. However, it's not just about creating a sitemap anymore. In the past, generating a site map acted as a roadmap for a website, detailing all its pages to aid users and search engines in navigating through its content. Now it's different, let's explore the fundamental elements of crafting SEO-optimized content, beginning with keyword research.

Keyword research serves as the cornerstone of SEO-optimized content creation. It involves identifying the specific words and phrases —known as keywords— that users type into search engines when looking for information online. These keywords play a crucial role in determining a website's ranking in search engine results pages (SERPs) and attracting relevant traffic.

In igniting the keyword research journey, I first turned to the trusted Google Keyword Planner. This invaluable tool offered a wealth of insights into search volume, competition, and keyword variations, empowering me to pinpoint high-potential keywords pertinent to my niche. Simply by inputting primary keywords associated with my business, product, or service, I gained access to an extensive array of related keywords along with their corresponding search metrics.

Additionally, I explored other free tools such as Ubersuggest and Keyword Tool, which provided further keyword suggestions and insights to refine my strategy. For more advanced features and in-depth analysis, I also explored paid options like SEMrush and Ahrefs, which offered comprehensive keyword data, competitive analysis, and trend tracking capabilities.

When conducting keyword research, I adopted a strategic approach to identify keywords with optimal search volume and competition levels. I aimed to strike a balance between broad keywords with high search volume and specific long-tail keywords with lower competition. By diversifying my keyword portfolio and targeting a mix of broad and niche-specific keywords, I optimized my chances of ranking for relevant search queries and attracting qualified traffic to my website.

Furthermore, I leveraged Google Trends to gain deeper insights into keyword trends and seasonal variations. This valuable tool allowed me to track the popularity of specific keywords over time, identify emerging trends, and tailor my content strategy accordingly. By staying informed about shifts in user search behavior and industry trends, I remained agile and responsive in my approach to keyword targeting.

Once armed with a comprehensive list of target keywords, I strategically integrated them into my content creation process. Rather than resorting to keyword stuffing —a practice frowned upon by search engines— I focused on creating high-quality, informative, and engaging content that naturally incorporated target keywords. From blog posts and product descriptions to landing pages and meta tags, I ensured that every piece of content was optimized for relevant keywords while maintaining readability and user experience.

In addition to primary keywords, I also explored long-tail keywords which are specific phrases that cater to niche audience segments. Long-tail keywords often have lower search volume but higher intent, making them valuable assets for capturing targeted traffic and driving conversions. By identifying long-tail keyword opportunities related to my niche, I expanded my content reach and attracted highly motivated visitors with specific search queries.

Ensuring that keywords are strategically incorporated throughout your website is very important for optimizing its visibility and search engine rankings. These keywords should seamlessly weave through various elements, including meta descriptions, titles, sub-titles, and the website's content itself. For instance, if you're running a pet grooming business in New York City, incorporating keywords like "pet grooming services NYC" in your meta descriptions and titles can enhance your website's relevance for local searches. Linking these keywords to relevant pages within your site not only improves navigation but also signals to search engines the importance of those pages. This cohesive approach to keyword integration enhances both user experience and search engine optimization, ultimately driving organic traffic and boosting your website's online presence.

" It's a bonus if your domain name includes your primary keyword!"

As I continually refined my SEO-optimized content strategy, I kept a close eye on key performance metrics including keyword rankings, organic traffic, and user engagement. These metrics offer valuable insights into the effectiveness of my keyword targeting efforts and guide future content optimization strategies. To monitor keyword rankings, I utilized tools like SEMrush or Ahrefs, which provide detailed reports on keyword positions in search engine results pages (SERPs). For tracking organic traffic, Google Analytics is a reliable free option that offers comprehensive data on website traffic sources and user behavior. Additionally, tools like Moz or SimilarWeb offer insights into user engagement metrics such as bounce rate, time on page, and pages per session. By regularly monitoring these metrics and adjusting my content strategy accordingly, I ensured that my website remained competitive in the internet.

Writing SEO-optimized content is a multifaceted process that begins with strategic keyword research and culminates in the creation of high-quality, user-centric content. By understanding the nuances of keyword targeting, embracing long-tail keyword opportunities, and prioritizing user experience, I've been able to enhance my website's visibility, attract organic traffic, and achieve sustainable growth in search engine rankings.

Implementing SEM Strategies for Visibility

Implementing a search engine marketing (SEM) strategy is also a major aspect of any digital marketing journey, doing so has enable me to enhance visibility, drive targeted traffic, and achieve tangible results for my website. Let's explore the world of SEM and my strategies for maximizing visibility and engagement across search engine platforms.

Search Engine Marketing (SEM) is a comprehensive digital marketing strategy aimed at increasing a website's visibility in search engine results pages (SERPs) through both paid advertising and organic tactics. While SEM encompasses various approaches, its primary focus is on paid advertising campaigns that target specific keywords relevant to a business or website. One of the key components of SEM is Pay-Per-Click (PPC) advertising, where advertisers bid on keywords and pay a fee each time their ad is clicked. PPC ads typically appear at the top or bottom of search engine results pages, marked as "sponsored" or "ad," offering advertisers prominent visibility and the potential to drive immediate traffic to their websites.

In addition to PPC ads, SEM encompasses display advertising, a strategy where visual ads are placed on websites within a network of publishers. Providers like Google Display Network, Facebook Ads, and LinkedIn Ads offer platforms for displaying these ads, which can include banners, images, or interactive multimedia. These ads are strategically placed on websites that attract the target audience, allowing advertisers to broaden their reach beyond search engine results pages. Display advertising enhances brand visibility and drives traffic through visually engaging content, creating opportunities for advertisers to connect with their audience in a more dynamic and interactive manner. Other forms of paid promotion in SEM include social media advertising, where ads are displayed on social media platforms like Facebook, Instagram, and LinkedIn to target specific demographics, interests, and behaviors. Remarketing or retargeting campaigns are also common in SEM, where ads are shown to users who have previously visited a website, encouraging them to return and complete a desired action, such as making a purchase or signing up for a newsletter. By leveraging a combination of PPC, display ads, social media advertising, and remarketing campaigns, SEM offers a comprehensive approach to driving targeted traffic to websites and maximizing online visibility and conversion opportunities.

Here are some key strategies I've employed to leverage SEM for visibility and success:

1. **Keyword Research and Selection:** Before launching any SEM campaign, I conducted extensive keyword research to identify relevant search terms with high commercial intent. By targeting keywords that align with my business objectives and resonate with my target audience, I maximized the effectiveness of my ad campaigns and ensured optimal ROI. I focused on selecting a mix of broad, competitive keywords and

specific long-tail keywords to capture diverse audience segments and drive targeted traffic to my website.

2. **Ad Copy Optimization:** Crafting compelling ad copy is essential for capturing users' attention and driving clicks. I invested time and effort into writing concise, persuasive ad copy that highlighted the unique value propositions of my products or services. By incorporating relevant keywords, compelling calls-to-action, and engaging messaging, I increased the likelihood of users clicking on my ads and exploring my website further.

3. **Ad Positioning and Bidding Strategy:** Achieving optimal ad positioning in search engine results requires careful bidding strategy and ongoing optimization. I closely monitored ad performance metrics such as click-through rate (CTR), conversion rate, and cost-per-click (CPC) to assess the effectiveness of my bidding strategy. By adjusting bids based on keyword performance, competition levels, and budget considerations, I optimized ad positioning and maximized visibility in SERPs.

4. **Ad Extensions and Enhancements:** To enhance the visibility and appeal of my ads, I leveraged various ad extensions and enhancements offered by search engine platforms. These extensions, such as sitelinks, callouts, and structured snippets, allowed me to provide additional information, showcase product features, and encourage user engagement directly within

the ad. By incorporating relevant extensions tailored to my campaign objectives, I improved ad visibility and encouraged users to take action.
5. **Targeted Audience Segmentation:** Effective audience targeting is essential for reaching the right users with SEM campaigns. I segmented my target audience based on demographic attributes, interests, and online behaviors to deliver personalized ad experiences tailored to their needs and preferences. By refining audience targeting parameters and aligning ad content with specific audience segments, I maximized relevance and engagement, ultimately driving higher conversion rates and ROI.
6. **Performance Tracking and Optimization:** Continuous monitoring and optimization are critical components of successful SEM campaigns. I regularly tracked key performance indicators (KPIs) such as ad impressions, clicks, conversions, and ROI to evaluate campaign effectiveness and identify areas for improvement. By analyzing performance data, conducting A/B testing, and refining ad creative and targeting parameters, I iteratively optimized my SEM campaigns to achieve optimal results and drive continuous growth.

As evident from my experience, integrating SEM strategies has proven pivotal in elevating visibility, directing tailored traffic, and attaining marketing goals for my website. By optimizing my SEM campaigns, I've effectively garnered tangible outcomes. As I persist in refining my SEM approach and accommodating dynamic market shifts, my dedication to harnessing SEM as a potent instrument for augmenting online presence and stimulating conversions remains unwavering.

Building Quality Backlinks and Off-Page SEO

Building quality backlinks involves acquiring links from external websites to your own site. These backlinks act as "votes of confidence" from other websites, indicating to search engines that your content is valuable and worthy of citation. The more high-quality backlinks you have from authoritative and relevant websites, the higher your website's authority becomes in the eyes of search engines.

Authority, in the context of SEO, refers to the perceived trustworthiness, expertise, and credibility of a website in a particular subject area or industry. Websites with higher authority are more likely to rank higher in search engine results pages because search engines prioritize authoritative sources when delivering search results to users.

Ranking refers to the position of a website or webpage in search engine results pages for specific search queries. The goal of SEO is to improve the ranking of a website or webpage so that it appears higher in search results, ideally on the first page. A higher-ranking increases visibility and organic traffic to the website, leading to more opportunities for engagement and conversions.

Understanding the Importance of Backlinks

Backlinks, or inbound links, are hyperlinks originating from external websites that direct users to pages on your own website. Given that search engines view backlinks as indicators of credibility and authority, understanding their importance is crucial. Therefore, I encourage you to prioritize the establishment of a diverse collection of high-quality backlinks from reputable websites within your industry niche. Allow me to outline my six-point checklist for backlinks

1. **Strategic Link Building Tactics:** To acquire quality backlinks, I employed a variety of strategic link building tactics aimed at earning natural, relevant links from authoritative sources. These tactics included guest blogging, outreach to industry influencers and bloggers, participation in online forums and communities, listing on local business directories, and creation of shareable, link-worthy content such as infographics, guides, and case studies. By offering valuable insights, expertise, and resources to target audiences, I cultivated mutually beneficial relationships and earned backlinks from reputable websites with high domain authority.

2. **Focus on Relevance and Authority:** When building backlinks, I prioritized relevance and authority to ensure maximum impact on search engine rankings. I sought opportunities to acquire backlinks from websites within my industry niche or related topics such as trade organization sites, as these links carry greater weight and relevance in the eyes of search engines. Additionally, I targeted websites with high domain authority, as backlinks from authoritative sources are more valuable in boosting my website's credibility and ranking.

3. **Natural Link Acquisition Strategies:** Rather than resorting to manipulative or spammy tactics, I focused on natural link acquisition strategies that adhere to search engine guidelines and best practices. I emphasized the creation of high-quality, shareable content that naturally attracts links and engagement from users. By consistently producing valuable, informative, and compelling content, I earned organic backlinks from reputable websites and fostered a positive reputation within my industry.

> *"Encouraging your users to bookmark or share your content is a valuable strategy that shouldn't be overlooked."*

4. **Monitoring and Analyzing Backlink Profile:** Consistently monitoring and analyzing my backlink profile played a crucial role in evaluating the quality, diversity, and relevance of inbound links. I relied on a range of tools and analytics platforms to keep track of

backlink metrics like domain authority, anchor text distribution, and referring domains. A good software tool for monitoring and analyzing backlink profiles is Ahrefs. It provides comprehensive insights into backlink metrics such as domain authority, anchor text distribution, referring domains, and more. Other popular tools include Moz's Link Explorer, SEMrush, and Majestic. These tools offer various features to track backlinks, assess their quality, and identify opportunities for improvement in your backlink profile. This comprehensive approach allowed me to pinpoint and rectify any low-quality or spammy backlinks, ensuring a healthy backlink profile and minimizing the likelihood of penalties from search engines.

5. **Diversification of Anchor Text:** In optimizing my backlink profile, I diversified anchor text usage to ensure natural, organic link patterns and avoid over-optimization penalties. Rather than relying solely on exact-match anchor text (The clickable text in a hyperlink), I incorporated variations such as branded anchors, naked URLs, and generic phrases to maintain a balanced and natural link profile. This approach helped improve the relevance and contextuality of backlinks while reducing the risk of algorithmic penalties.

6. **Continuous Monitoring and Adaptation:** SEO is an ongoing process, and the landscape of backlink building is constantly evolving. I remained vigilant

and adaptive, continuously monitoring changes in search engine algorithms, industry trends, and competitor strategies. By staying informed and proactive, I was able to adapt my link building tactics, refine my off-page SEO strategies, and maintain a competitive edge in the ever-changing SEO world.

Building quality backlinks and optimizing off-page elements are essential components of a comprehensive SEO strategy aimed at improving search engine rankings, increasing organic traffic, and enhancing online visibility.

"Build back links from .EDU school websites, and .GOV government sites to gain extra credibility and rank."

Leveraging Social Media for SEO Benefits

Integrating social media into SEO strategies has become an indispensable component of modern digital marketing endeavors. Through strategic alignment with social media platforms, I've witnessed firsthand the profound impact on brand visibility, organic traffic generation, and search engine ranking enhancement. By orchestrating a harmonious synergy between social media engagement and SEO initiatives, I've unlocked new avenues for reaching and engaging with target audiences while bolstering the overall online presence of my brand.

Social signals, including likes, shares, comments, and engagement metrics on social media platforms, are pivotal indicators of a website's credibility and relevance. These signals reflect the level of interaction and endorsement that content receives from users within the social sphere. Essentially, they represent the digital footprint of how users perceive and engage with the content shared on various social media platforms. By actively engaging with the audience and fostering meaningful interactions, website owners can cultivate a strong social media presence and generate social signals that signify trustworthiness and authority to search engines. As search algorithms increasingly consider social signals when ranking websites, prioritizing social media engagement has become integral to enhancing online visibility and credibility.

Social media serves as a powerful channel for amplifying the reach and visibility of any website's content. Whenever I publish new blog posts, articles, infographics, or multimedia content on my website, I leverage social media to disseminate and promote that content to a wider audience. By sharing compelling and relevant content across my social media profiles, I've been able to drive traffic back to my website for free, attract new visitors, and increase the likelihood of earning backlinks from social media users and influencers. Remember backlinks are an important part of SEO and SERPs ranking.

Optimized Social Profiles and Link Building

I strategically enhanced my social media profiles by incorporating pertinent keywords, branded visuals, and links to my website, amplifying their discoverability and SEO significance. I've also leveraged hashtags to ensure that my content reached relevant audiences and garnered visibility across platforms. Each social media profile serves as a pivotal digital asset, enriching my online footprint and fortifying link-building endeavors. By integrating website URLs into bios, posts, and profile descriptions, I've cultivated supplementary avenues for users to seamlessly access my website, thus augmenting referral traffic and reinforcing my website's credibility and authority with search engines.

Engagement and Community Building

Building an engaged and loyal community of followers on social media has been instrumental in driving SEO benefits. I prioritize meaningful interactions, conversations, and engagement with my audience to foster a sense of community and brand loyalty. By responding promptly to comments, messages, and inquiries, I've nurtured positive relationships with followers and influencers, thereby increasing the likelihood of social sharing, brand advocacy, and organic amplification of my website's content.

Social Sharing and Virality

Encouraging social sharing and virality of my website's content has been a cornerstone of my social media strategy. I create shareable, visually appealing, and engaging content that resonates with my target audience and prompts users to share it with their social networks. By leveraging social sharing buttons, plugins, and incentives, I've facilitated easy sharing of my content across various social platforms, amplifying its reach and virality. Viral content has the potential to attract a surge of traffic, generate buzz, and earn valuable backlinks from authoritative websites, thereby boosting SEO performance.

Crafting viral marketing promotion techniques requires a blend of creativity, strategy, and timing to capture the attention of audiences and spark organic sharing across digital channels. This could entail creating entertaining videos, humorous memes, inspiring stories, or thought-provoking infographics that evoke strong emotions and compel viewers to engage and share with their networks.

Another strategy is to harness the power of user-generated content and social proof to fuel virality. Encouraging users to participate in challenges, contests, or campaigns where they create and share content related to your brand or product can amplify reach and engagement. By incentivizing participation with rewards, recognition, or exclusive access, you can motivate users to become brand advocates and amplify your message organically. Additionally, leveraging influencer partnerships and collaborations can extend your reach to new audiences and lend credibility and authenticity to your viral marketing efforts. Through strategic partnerships with influencers who align with your brand values and resonate with your target demographic, you can amplify your message and foster widespread sharing and engagement.

Social Listening and Insights

It's crucial to emphasize the depth of understanding that can be gained from monitoring social media platforms. Social listening tools, such as Brandwatch, Hootsuite Insights, and Mention, enable me to track not only direct mentions of my brand but also broader conversations related to my industry, products, or services. By analyzing these conversations, I can uncover emerging trends, identify common pain points or desires among my target audience, and stay ahead of the curve in terms of content creation and optimization.

Moreover, social media insights provide quantitative data that complements qualitative insights gathered through social listening. Analytics platforms like Facebook Insights, Twitter Analytics, and LinkedIn Analytics offer metrics such as engagement rates, audience demographics, and content performance, allowing me to measure the effectiveness of my social media efforts and identify areas for improvement. For example, I can track which types of content resonate most with my audience, the best times to post for maximum visibility, and the demographics of my most engaged followers.

By combining both social listening and insights, I can fine-tune my SEO strategy to better meet the needs and preferences of my audience. For instance, if I notice a spike in conversations around a particular topic on social media using tools like BuzzSumo or Sprout Social, I can create targeted content optimized for relevant keywords to capitalize on the trend and drive organic traffic to my website. Similarly, if social media insights reveal that a certain demographic engages more with visual content, I can prioritize the creation of engaging visuals in my SEO content strategy.

In essence, social listening and insights serve as invaluable tools for optimizing SEO strategies by providing real-time feedback, identifying opportunities for content optimization, and ensuring alignment with audience interests and preferences. By leveraging these insights effectively, I've been able to stay agile in my approach to SEO and maintain a competitive edge.

CHAPTER 10 - MONETIZATION TACTICS

Maximizing Revenue with Google AdWords

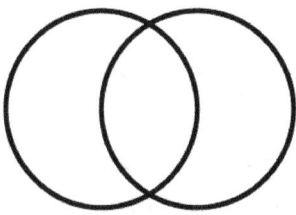

As I delved deeper into the world of online monetization, one of the most powerful tools I encountered was Google AdWords. This platform, offered by the search engine giant, provided an incredible opportunity to maximize revenue by strategically placing ads across the vast landscape of the internet.

My journey with Google AdWords or now Google Ads began with a sense of curiosity and a desire to explore new avenues for generating income through my website. I had heard countless success stories from other website owners who had leveraged AdWords to significantly boost their revenue streams, and I was eager to experience similar results for myself.

The first step in my AdWords journey was to familiarize myself with the platform and its various features. Google AdWords offers a comprehensive suite of tools and resources designed to help advertisers create, manage, and optimize their ad campaigns with ease. From keyword research tools to advanced targeting options, AdWords provided everything I needed to launch successful ad campaigns tailored to my specific goals and objectives.

One of the key benefits of Google AdWords is its ability to target highly relevant audiences based on their search queries and online behavior. By carefully selecting keywords related to my niche and crafting compelling ad copy, I was able to connect with users who were actively searching for products or services like mine. This targeted approach not only increased the effectiveness of my ads but also maximized the return on investment for my advertising budget.

As I began to experiment with different ad formats and placement strategies, I quickly realized the importance of tracking and analyzing the performance of my campaigns. Google AdWords provides robust analytics and reporting tools that allow advertisers to monitor the success of their ads in real-time. By closely monitoring metrics such as click-through rates, conversion rates, and cost-per-click, I was able to identify which ads were generating the best results and adjust my strategies accordingly.

One of the most powerful features of Google AdWords is its ability to scale campaigns based on performance. As I gained more experience with the platform and refined my targeting strategies, I gradually increased my ad spend to reach a larger audience and drive more traffic to my website. With AdWords, I had the flexibility to adjust my budget and bidding strategy in real-time, allowing me to maximize the impact of my advertising efforts.

In addition to traditional search ads, Google AdWords also offers a variety of other ad formats, including display ads, video ads, and shopping ads. By diversifying my advertising portfolio and experimenting with different formats, I was able to reach users across multiple channels and capture their attention at various stages of the buying cycle.

Overall, my experience with Google AdWords was nothing short of transformative. Through strategic planning, careful execution, and continuous optimization, I was able to maximize revenue and grow my online business to new heights.

" Pay special attention to the text of your ads."

Exploring Diverse Monetization Methods

As I delved deeper into the world of online entrepreneurship, I realized that relying solely on a single monetization method was limiting the potential revenue streams of my website. To truly maximize earnings and diversify my income sources, I began exploring a wide range of monetization methods that would complement each other and provide multiple streams of revenue.

One of the first alternative monetization methods I explored was affiliate marketing. This approach involved partnering with other companies and promoting their products or services on my website in exchange for a commission on sales generated through affiliate links. Affiliate marketing, facilitated through networks like Amazon Associates, offered a flexible and scalable way to monetize my website, allowing me to earn passive income by recommending products and services that aligned with my audience's interests and needs. Through affiliate partnerships, I could leverage the credibility and trust I had built with my audience to promote relevant products or services. This not only provided a steady stream of income but also added value to my audience by offering them access to quality products or services that I personally endorsed.

In addition to affiliate marketing, I also began exploring sponsored content and sponsored reviews as a means of monetization. By collaborating with brands and advertisers to create sponsored posts or reviews, I was able to generate revenue while providing valuable content to my audience. Sponsored content allowed me to monetize my expertise and knowledge in my niche while maintaining transparency and authenticity with my readers.

Another monetization method I explored was premium content and membership subscriptions. I created exclusive premium content, such as in-depth guides, tutorials, or downloadable resources, and offered them to my audience as part of a membership subscription package. By providing additional value and exclusive access to premium content, I was able to attract subscribers willing to pay a premium fee for access to exclusive benefits and resources.

As I continued looking for monetization methods, I ventured into the world of digital products and online courses as a means of monetizing my expertise and skills. I created and launched digital products such as e-books, templates, or software tools that addressed specific pain points or challenges faced by my audience. Additionally, I developed online courses and training programs that offered comprehensive learning experiences and valuable insights into my niche industry.

Eventually, I realized the importance of experimenting and adapting my strategies based on the evolving needs and preferences of my audience. Each monetization method had its own strengths and limitations, and it was essential to find the right balance and combination of methods that would yield the highest return on investment.

Ultimately, by exploring diverse monetization methods and embracing a multi-faceted approach to revenue generation, I was able to unlock new income streams and maximize the earning potential of my website. Diversifying my monetization strategies not only increased my overall revenue but also provided greater stability and resilience against fluctuations in market conditions and changes in consumer behavior.

Developing and Managing Affiliate Programs

Embarking on the journey of developing and managing affiliate programs opened up a realm of possibilities for expanding my revenue streams. Affiliate programs provided a mutually beneficial arrangement where both the affiliates (me) and the merchants (companies whose products or services I promoted) could leverage each other's strengths to drive sales and generate revenue.

The process of developing an affiliate program began with identifying suitable merchants whose products or services resonated with my audience and aligned with the themes of my website. This involved conducting thorough research to identify reputable companies with high-quality offerings and affiliate programs that offered competitive commissions and incentives.

Online Magic

Once I had identified potential merchant partners, I reached out to them to express my interest in joining their affiliate programs. Many merchants had dedicated affiliate program portals or sign-up pages where I could apply to become an affiliate. In some cases, I had to submit an application and await approval from the merchant before gaining access to their affiliate program resources.

Upon approval, I gained access to a variety of promotional materials and resources provided by the merchant, including affiliate links, banners, product images, and marketing collateral. These materials were essential for effectively promoting the merchant's products or services on my website and driving traffic to their website or landing pages.

One of the key aspects of managing affiliate programs was tracking and monitoring performance metrics to evaluate the effectiveness of my promotional efforts and optimize my strategies for maximum results. Most affiliate programs provided affiliate dashboards or tracking tools that allowed me to monitor clicks, conversions, sales, and commissions in real-time.

In addition to monitoring performance metrics, I also focused on building strong relationships with my merchant partners and providing value-added services to support their affiliate marketing efforts. This involved communicating regularly with merchant representatives, providing feedback and insights, and collaborating on promotional campaigns and initiatives.

As my affiliate partnerships grew, I explored various strategies for maximizing affiliate revenue and optimizing conversion rates. This included experimenting with different promotional tactics, optimizing affiliate links and landing pages for better conversion rates, and leveraging analytics data to identify trends and opportunities for improvement.

I prioritized transparency and authenticity in my affiliate marketing efforts by clearly disclosing my affiliate relationships to my audience and providing honest and unbiased recommendations and reviews of the products or services I promoted. Building trust and credibility with my audience was paramount to the success of my affiliate marketing endeavors.

Overall, developing and managing affiliate programs proved to be a lucrative and rewarding venture, allowing me to forge valuable partnerships, diversify my revenue streams, and create mutually beneficial relationships with merchants and affiliates alike.

Converting Website Traffic into Sales Leads

Converting website traffic into sales leads is a crucial aspect of maximizing the revenue potential of any online business. While attracting visitors to my website was crucial, it was equally important to engage and convert them into qualified leads who were primed for further interaction and eventual conversion into paying customers.

The process of converting website traffic into sales leads involved a strategic combination of targeted marketing tactics, compelling content, and optimized lead generation strategies. Here's how I approached this essential aspect of my online business:

1. **Understanding Audience Needs**: As we saw in past chapters, the first step in converting website traffic into sales leads is gaining a deep understanding of our target audience's needs, preferences, and pain points. By conducting thorough market research and analyzing visitor behavior on my website, I gained valuable insights into what motivated them and how I could address their needs effectively.
2. **Creating Compelling Content**: Content played a central role in attracting and engaging website visitors, as well as nurturing them through the sales funnel. I focused on creating high-quality, informative, and engaging content that resonated with my target audience and provided them with valuable insights, solu-

tions, and resources related to their interests and challenges.

3. **Implementing Lead Capture Mechanisms**: To capture website visitors' information and convert them into leads, I implemented various lead capture mechanisms, such as opt-in forms, pop-ups, gated content, and interactive tools. These mechanisms encouraged visitors to provide their contact information in exchange for valuable content, such as e-books, guides, webinars, or exclusive offers.

4. **Segmenting and Personalizing Communication**: Once I captured the leads' contact information, I segmented them based on their interests, behaviors, and demographics to deliver personalized and relevant communication. By tailoring my messaging to their specific needs and preferences, I could nurture leads more effectively and guide them through the sales funnel towards conversion.

5. **Implementing Lead Nurturing Campaigns**: Lead nurturing campaigns played a crucial role in building relationships with leads over time and moving them closer to conversion. Through a series of automated emails, targeted content, and personalized interactions, I provided leads with valuable information, addressed their concerns, and positioned my products or services as solutions to their needs.

6. **Utilizing Retargeting Strategies**: Retargeting strategies allowed me to re-engage website visitors who had shown interest in my products or services but had not

yet converted into leads. By serving them targeted ads or personalized content based on their previous interactions with my website, I could keep my brand top-of-mind and encourage them to take the next step towards becoming a lead.

> *"Tracking analytics is crucial for your website, especially due to the significance of retargeting."*

7. **Measuring and Optimizing Performance**: Continuous measurement and optimization were essential for refining my lead generation strategies and maximizing their effectiveness. I tracked key performance indicators (KPIs) such as conversion rates, lead quality, and customer acquisition costs to identify areas for improvement and fine-tune my approach over time.

By implementing these strategies and focusing on converting website traffic into sales leads, you'll be able to build a robust pipeline of qualified leads and drive sustained growth and profitability for your online business. Each interaction with website visitors presents an opportunity to nurture relationships, provide value, and ultimately guide them towards becoming loyal customers. It's not easy, and it will require a lot of A/B testing to find the right funnel. However, once the right funnel has been put in to place, income will just start to come in on auto pilot.

Creating and Selling Digital Products

In my experience creating and selling digital products has been a significant milestone in my journey to diversify monetization tactics and maximizing revenue streams. Unlike physical products, digital products offered scalability, low overhead costs, and the potential for recurring revenue, making them an attractive option for generating passive income.

I've tried many types of products and various ways to sell them, and undoubtedly, selling through a website is the most attractive because you save on all the costs of having a traditional business. Additionally, you'll always have the opportunity to setup affiliate marketing and referrals processes to increase your sales.

Here's how I approached the process of creating and selling digital products:

1. **Identifying Marketable Ideas**: The first step in creating digital products was identifying marketable ideas that aligned with my expertise, audience's interests, and market demand. I conducted thorough market research, analyzed industry trends, and solicited feedback from my audience to pinpoint topics or solutions that addressed their needs and pain points.
2. **Choosing the Right Format**: Digital products come in various formats, including e-books, online courses,

templates, software, digital downloads, audio, and video files. I evaluated the strengths and limitations of each format and selected the ones that best suited the content and delivery method of my digital product. For example, if I wanted to teach a comprehensive course on digital marketing, an online course platform would be ideal for delivering video lessons, quizzes, and interactive content.

3. **Content Creation and Development**: Once I had a clear idea of the digital product's concept and format, I focused on creating high-quality content that provided value and addressed the target audience's needs. Whether it was writing an e-book, recording video tutorials, or designing templates, I ensured that the content was well-researched, organized, and presented in a visually appealing manner.

4. **Designing Engaging Sales Pages**: A compelling sales page is essential for effectively promoting digital products and convincing potential customers to make a purchase. I invested time and effort into designing engaging sales pages that highlighted the benefits of the digital product, showcased testimonials or case studies, and included persuasive call-to-action buttons to encourage conversions.

5. **Setting Competitive Pricing**: Pricing digital products requires careful consideration of factors such as production costs, perceived value, competitor pricing, and market demand. I conducted pricing research to determine the optimal price point that balanced prof-

itability with affordability for my target audience. Additionally, I experimented with pricing strategies such as tiered pricing, discounts, or bundling to incentivize purchases and maximize revenue.

6. **Implementing Secure Payment Processing**: To facilitate seamless transactions and ensure customer trust, I integrated secure payment processing systems into my e-commerce platform. I selected reputable payment gateways that supported various payment methods, offered encryption for sensitive data, and complied with industry standards for security and fraud prevention.

7. **Promoting and Marketing Digital Products**: Effective promotion and marketing were essential for driving traffic to my sales pages and generating sales for my digital products. I utilized a combination of digital marketing channels, including email marketing, social media, content marketing, and search engine optimization (SEO), to reach my target audience, build awareness, and encourage conversions. Additionally, I leveraged partnerships, affiliate marketing programs, and influencer collaborations to expand my reach and tap into new customer segments.

8. **Providing Ongoing Support and Updates**: Customer satisfaction and retention were paramount in the digital product business. I provided excellent customer support to address inquiries, resolve issues, and assist customers throughout their purchase journey. Additionally, I regularly updated and improved my digital

products based on customer feedback, market trends, and technological advancements to ensure continued value and relevance.

By following these steps and leveraging digital platforms and marketing strategies, I successfully created and sold digital products that catered to my audience's needs, generated passive income, and diversified my revenue streams. Digital products not only provided a scalable and profitable monetization option but also positioned me as an authority in my niche and facilitated long-term relationships with customers.

> *"I've followed these steps every time I start something new, and I've done well every time."*

Implementing Subscription-Based Models

In my opinion, implementing subscription-based models is the best way to monetize a website and cultivate sustainable revenue streams. Embracing this model allowed me to offer valuable recurring services or content to subscribers while fostering long-term relationships and predictable revenue.

Before diving into subscription-based offerings, I gained a comprehensive understanding of the subscription model and its various components. I researched different subscription models, such as product subscriptions, membership subscriptions, and software as a service (SaaS) subscription, to determine which model best suited my business objectives, target audience, and industry trends.

Next, I identified subscription opportunities within my niche or industry that aligned with my expertise, audience's needs, and market demand. I conducted market research, analyzed competitor offerings, and solicited feedback from my audience to pinpoint potential subscription services, products, or content that could provide ongoing value and justify recurring payments.

To create compelling subscription offerings, I defined subscription tiers with different levels of access, benefits, and pricing options to cater to diverse customer segments and budgets. I carefully crafted pricing strategies based on factors such as the perceived value of the subscription, competitor pricing, production costs, and target market's willingness to pay. Additionally, I experimented with free trials, introductory discounts, and annual subscription plans to incentivize sign-ups and boost retention.

The key to successful subscription-based models is delivering ongoing value and engagement to subscribers. I focused on developing high-quality and exclusive content, services, or features that were not available elsewhere and provided tangible benefits to subscribers. Whether it was premium content, access to online communities, personalized services, or software updates, I ensured that subscribers received continuous value that justified their subscription investment.

Creating Seamless Subscription Experiences

A seamless user experience is essential for attracting and retaining subscribers. I invested in user-friendly subscription management platforms or e-commerce systems that facilitated easy sign-ups, subscription management, payment processing, and account access for subscribers. Additionally, I optimized subscription workflows, checkout processes, and customer communication to minimize friction and enhance satisfaction throughout the subscriber journey.

Retaining subscribers is crucial for the long-term success of subscription-based models. I implemented retention strategies such as proactive customer support, personalized recommendations, loyalty rewards, and engagement campaigns to nurture relationships with subscribers, encourage renewals, and reduce churn. By continuously monitoring subscriber engagement, satisfaction, and retention metrics, I identified opportunities for improvement and adjusted strategies accordingly to maximize subscriber lifetime value.

As my subscriber base grew, I focused on scaling and diversifying subscription offerings to accommodate evolving customer needs and preferences. I introduced new subscription tiers, expanded content libraries or service offerings, and explored partnerships or collaborations to enhance value propositions and attract new subscribers. Additionally, I leveraged data analytics, customer feedback, and market insights to refine subscription strategies, optimize pricing models, and drive continuous growth.

Ensuring Compliance and Security

As I mentioned in previous chapters, compliance with data protection regulations, such as the General Data Protection Regulation (GDPR) or the California Consumer Privacy Act (CCPA), was paramount in managing subscription-based models. I implemented robust data security measures, obtained necessary consent for data processing, and ensured transparency in data handling practices to maintain subscriber trust and comply with legal requirements. In this way, I maintain peace of mind and ensure that I am complying with legal regulations to protect my customers.

Additionally, by strategically implementing subscription-based models, I transformed one-time transactions into recurring revenue streams, fostered loyal customer relationships, and established a resilient foundation for sustainable business growth. Subscription offerings not only provided ongoing value to subscribers but also diversified revenue sources, reduced dependency on single transactions, and enabled continuous innovation and adaptation to changing market dynamics.

Offering Premium Content and Memberships

Offering premium content and memberships are a great way to monetize online platforms, by providing exclusive value and access to users.

Always begin by identifying valuable content or resources within your niche that have the potential to attract a dedicated audience willing to pay for exclusive access. This could include in-depth guides, tutorials, courses, webinars, e-books, templates, or industry insights that offer unique insights, expertise, or solutions to specific challenges faced by your target audience.

Once you have identified premium content opportunities, focus on creating high-quality, in-depth, and actionable content that provides tangible value and addresses specific pain points or aspirations of your audience. Leverage your expertise, research, and use creativity to develop premium content that is not readily available elsewhere and offer a competitive edge to subscribers.

In addition to premium content, you can create membership programs that offer exclusive benefits, perks, and privileges to subscribers. Define different membership tiers with varying levels of access, features, and pricing options to cater to diverse customer segments and budgets. These membership benefits could include ad-free browsing, early access to content, exclusive community forums, member-only events, discounts on products or services, and personalized support.

To streamline subscription management and deliver a seamless user experience, you can implement subscription or membership platforms that facilitate easy sign-ups, recurring billing, access management, and member communication. These platforms integrated with your website, will allow subscribers to register, upgrade or downgrade their memberships, and access exclusive content or benefits with ease. And at the same time most of these platforms will provide you with easy administration sections for your accounting needs.

Develop comprehensive marketing strategies to promote premium content and memberships to your target audience. This involves leveraging various marketing channels such as email marketing, social media promotion, content marketing, and paid advertising to raise awareness, drive traffic, and encourage sign-ups for premium content or membership programs. Highlight the unique value proposition, benefits, and features of premium offerings to entice potential subscribers and differentiate them from free content.

To retain subscribers and encourage renewals, prioritize providing exceptional value and support to premium content subscribers and members. This includes regularly updating and refreshing premium content to keep it relevant and valuable, responding promptly to member inquiries or feedback, and fostering a sense of community and belonging among members through engagement initiatives and exclusive events.

Continuously monitor the performance of premium content and membership programs using analytics tools, subscriber feedback, and key performance indicators (KPIs) such as subscriber growth, retention rates, revenue generated, and engagement metrics. Based on these insights, you can optimize strategies to improve subscriber satisfaction, retention, and revenue generation over time.

Always be compliant with data protection regulations, ensuring the security of member data is paramount in managing premium content and membership programs. Implemented robust data security measures, obtain necessary consent for data processing, and maintain transparency in data handling practices to safeguard member privacy and comply with legal requirements.

By offering premium content and memberships, you can not only diversify your revenue streams but also provide exclusive value to your audience, foster deeper relationships with subscribers, and establish a sustainable foundation for long-term growth and success. These premium offerings will allow you to monetize your expertise, creativity, and unique insights while empowering your audience to achieve their goals and aspirations.

Monetizing Email Newsletters and Lists

Monetizing email newsletters and lists has been a great source of income for some of the projects I've worked on, and have also been a great way to engage with my audience on a deeper level.

I started by building a substantial email list composed of engaged subscribers interested in receiving valuable content, updates, and offers related to my niche. Then I employed various strategies such as offering lead magnets, opt-in incentives, and engaging content to encourage website visitors to subscribe to my email newsletter.

"Aggressively Ask for Email Sign-ups"

To maintain subscriber engagement and trust, I consistently delivered high-quality, relevant, and valuable content in my email newsletters. This content included informative articles, helpful tips, industry insights, exclusive offers, product recommendations, and personalized recommendations tailored to the interests and preferences of my subscribers. I also segmented my email list based on subscriber demographics, preferences, behaviors, and engagement levels to deliver targeted and personalized content that resonated with different audience segments. By understanding the unique needs and interests of each segment, I could tailor my email marketing campaigns and offers to maximize relevance and effectiveness.

Strategically integrating affiliate marketing into my email newsletters allowed me to promote relevant products or services to my subscribers and earning commissions for qualified referrals or sales. I carefully selected affiliate products or programs that aligned with the interests and needs of my audience and disclosed any affiliate relationships transparently to maintain trust and credibility.

Selling sponsored content or advertising placements to relevant brands or businesses looking to reach my audience allowed me to earn that income I was looking for. I negotiated partnerships and sponsorship deals with brands that offered value to my subscribers and integrated sponsored content seamlessly into my newsletters to maintain a positive user experience.

I've also introduced premium subscription tiers or membership programs for email newsletters, offering exclusive content, perks, or benefits to subscribers who opted for paid subscriptions. These premium offerings provided additional value and incentives for subscribers to upgrade their subscriptions while generating recurring revenue for my business. Leveraging email newsletters, I promoted products, services, courses, or events to subscribers, highlighting the unique features, benefits, and value propositions of my offerings. I used compelling call-to-actions to encourage subscribers to make purchases or engage further with my brand. Next to continuously monitoring and optimizing the performance of my email marketing campaigns using analytics tools, A/B testing, and performance metrics such as open rates, click-through rates, conversion rates, and revenue generated, I iterated on my strategies based on data-driven insights to improve engagement, conversion, and monetization over time.

By monetizing email newsletters and lists, I not only generated additional revenue streams but also strengthened relationships with my audience, enhanced brand visibility, and drove conversions and sales. This strategy allowed me to leverage the power of email marketing to connect with my audience on a personal level while achieving my goals.

Hosting Webinars and Online Courses

Hosting webinars and online courses emerged as a need for a new marketing strategy, allowing me to share valuable knowledge, engage with my audience, and generate revenue. Here's a glimpse into my approach to hosting webinars and crafting online courses to capitalize on this opportunity.

I began by conducting market research and analyzing audience feedback to identify topics and themes that resonated with my target audience and aligned with their interests, needs, and pain points. By understanding my audience's preferences and challenges, I could develop webinar and course topics that offered practical solutions and valuable insights. I carefully planned and structured the content for my webinars and online courses to deliver comprehensive and actionable information in a clear, organized, and engaging format. I outlined key learning objectives, created detailed lesson plans, and curated relevant resources, examples, and case studies to enhance the learning experience for participants.

Selecting the right format and delivery method is also important, there are various formats and delivery methods for hosting webinars and online courses, including live webinars, pre-recorded videos, interactive workshops, downloadable resources, and multimedia presentations. Depending on the topic and audience preferences, I usually chose the most suitable format to maximize engagement and learning outcomes.

To promote and market I developed a comprehensive marketing strategy to promote my webinars and online courses and attract participants. This strategy included leveraging various marketing channels such as email marketing, social media, content marketing, paid advertising, influencer partnerships, and affiliate marketing to reach a wider audience and drive registrations.

"Having the right content generating team for this is key!"

A range of free and paid options were available for my webinars and online courses, designed to address the diverse needs of audience segments and meet various monetization goals. Free offerings served as lead generation tools to attract new prospects and build credibility, while paid options provided premium content, advanced training, and exclusive benefits for monetization. I created compelling sales pages and landing pages to promote my webinars and online courses and encourage registrations or purchases. These pages highlighted the key benefits, features, and value propositions of the offerings and included persuasive copywriting, testimonials, visuals, and calls-to-action to drive conversions.

During live webinars and online course sessions, I focused on delivering engaging, interactive, and value-packed content to keep participants actively involved and motivated. I encouraged audience interaction through polls, Q&A sessions, discussions, group activities, and live demonstrations to foster a sense of community and facilitate learning.

Ongoing support and resources to participants enrolled in my online courses, including access to course materials, supplementary resources, discussion forums, and mentorship opportunities was always offered. By providing comprehensive support and guidance, I enhanced the learning experience and helped participants achieve their goals.

After each webinar or course session, I collected feedback from participants to gather insights, evaluate performance, and identify areas for improvement. I used participant feedback to iterate on future sessions, refine content, address concerns, and enhance the overall learning experience.

As demand for my webinars and online courses grew, I scaled my offerings by creating additional courses, expanding topic coverage, and diversifying content formats. I continuously monitored market trends, audience preferences, and industry developments to stay relevant and competitive in the online education space.

Hosting webinars and creating online courses allowed me to share my expertise, connect with my audience which is key for internet businesses, and generate revenue while providing valuable learning opportunities for participants. This monetization strategy not only diversified my income streams but also positioned me as a trusted authority in my niche and contributed to the long-term success of my business at the time.

Leveraging Sponsored Content and Paid Reviews

Leveraging sponsored content and paid reviews has been a strategic approach I've implemented to monetize different websites not just my websites but those of clients, while providing valuable exposure to brands and products relevant to its different audiences.

This is done by Identifying relevant brands, partnerships and companies whose products or services align with the interests, needs, and preferences of the target audience. By selecting relevant partners, I ensure that sponsored content and paid reviews resonate with my target audience and provide genuine value.

Before engaging in sponsored content or paid reviews, I establish clear guidelines and standards to maintain transparency, authenticity, and integrity. I communicate these guidelines to potential partners to ensure mutual understanding and alignment with my brand values and audience expectations. I also focus on delivering informative, engaging, and authentic narratives that resonate with my audience and showcase the value proposition of the sponsored products or services. I strive to maintain editorial independence while effectively integrating sponsored messaging into the content.

While sponsored content provides an opportunity for monetization, maintaining editorial integrity is paramount. I ensure that sponsored content is clearly disclosed to my audience and clearly differentiated from editorial content to avoid any confusion or misrepresentation. I have known that some people try to hide the sponsored content within the content so that it is confused and has more clicks, however this practice can often give undesirable results on the long run.

Providing Value to Brands and Partners

I collaborate closely with brands and partners to understand their objectives, target audience, and key messaging. By aligning with their goals and providing value through sponsored content and paid reviews, I build strong and mutually beneficial relationships that lead to long-term partnerships and repeat business. Leveraging multiple platforms, and content formats to maximize the reach and impact of sponsored content and paid reviews. This includes blog posts, articles, videos, podcasts, social media posts, and newsletters, allowing me to engage with the audience across different channels and touchpoints.

Transparency is essential in sponsored content and paid reviews. I always disclose any sponsored partnerships or compensated reviews to my audience to maintain trust and credibility. Clear and upfront disclosure helps foster transparency and integrity.

Monitoring and Measuring Performance
Regularly monitor and measure the performance of sponsored content and paid reviews to assess their impact, effectiveness, and ROI. Key performance indicators (KPIs) may include audience engagement, brand awareness, click-through rates, conversions, and overall campaign success.

In addition to tracking key performance indicators (KPIs), it's essential to analyze audience feedback and sentiment regarding sponsored content and paid reviews. Utilize tools like social media listening platforms and surveys to gather insights into how your audience perceives and engages with sponsored content. Pay attention to comments, shares, and reactions to gauge sentiment and identify areas for improvement or optimization.

Furthermore, consider the long-term impact of sponsored content and paid reviews on your brand reputation and credibility. While immediate metrics like click-through rates and conversions are important, maintaining authenticity and trust with your audience is paramount.

Continuously evaluate the alignment between sponsored content and your brand values to ensure consistency and authenticity in your messaging. Building strong relationships with your audience based on transparency and integrity will ultimately drive sustainable success in your monetization efforts.

Adhering to Legal and Regulatory Requirements

Always ensure compliance with relevant legal and regulatory requirements, including disclosure guidelines set forth by regulatory bodies such as the Federal Trade Commission (FTC). By adhering to these guidelines, you can mitigate the risk of potential legal issues and maintain ethical standards in sponsored content and paid reviews.

Before entering into sponsored content or paid review partnerships, conduct thorough due diligence to evaluate the credibility, reputation, and alignment of potential partners with brand values and audience interests. This helps ensure that partnerships are mutually beneficial and conducive to long-term success.

This monetization strategy not only drives revenue but also strengthens relationships with partners and enhances the overall quality and relevance of content offerings.

Taking payments Online

Setting up an online store involves more than just showcasing products or services; it's about creating a seamless experience for customers to browse, select, and purchase items with ease. A pivotal aspect of this process is implementing an efficient payment system that ensures transactions are secure, convenient, and hassle-free.

When it comes to building your online store, choosing the right website builder is crucial. DomainCart.com offers an easy-to-use online store website builder product (https://app.domaincart.com/products/website-builder) that provides a robust platform for creating and managing your e-commerce website. With customizable templates and intuitive drag-and-drop functionality, you can design a professional-looking online store tailored to your brand's aesthetic and style.

In addition to DomainCart.com's online store website builder, there are other popular options available in the market, such as WordPress with WooCommerce integration. WordPress is a widely used content management system (CMS) known for its flexibility and versatility, while WooCommerce is a powerful e-commerce plugin specifically designed for WordPress. Together, they offer a comprehensive solution for building and managing your online store, providing access to a vast library of themes, plugins, and extensions to customize your store's functionality and design to meet your specific needs.

Online Magic

WordPress with WooCommerce allows you to leverage the full potential of WordPress's blogging capabilities alongside robust e-commerce features. You can easily create product listings, manage inventory, process orders, and accept payments through various payment gateways. The platform also offers extensive customization options, allowing you to tailor your store's design, layout, and functionality to align with your brand identity and business goals.

With WordPress and WooCommerce, you have the flexibility to scale your online store as your business grows. Whether you're selling physical products, digital downloads, or services, WordPress and WooCommerce provide a user-friendly and scalable solution to launch and manage your e-commerce business effectively. Additionally, the platform's extensive community support and documentation make it easy to find resources and assistance to optimize your online store for success.

Once your e-commerce website is up and running, the next step is to integrate a reliable payment gateway that allows you to accept payments from customers. Stripe (https://stripe.com/) is a popular choice among online businesses due to its user-friendly interface, advanced security features, and seamless integration capabilities.

While Stripe offers numerous benefits for processing online payments, including support for major credit cards, seamless checkout experiences, and robust fraud prevention tools, it's not the only option available. Other reputable payment gateways, such as PayPal, Square, and Authorize.Net, also offer a range of features and pricing options to meet the needs of different businesses.

When selecting a payment gateway for your online store, consider factors such as transaction fees, processing times, supported payment methods, and security features. Additionally, ensure that the payment gateway complies with industry regulations and standards for data security, such as PCI DSS (Payment Card Industry Data Security Standard) compliance.

Once you've chosen a website builder and integrated a payment gateway, it's essential to optimize your online store's checkout process for maximum efficiency and convenience. Streamline the checkout flow by minimizing the number of steps required to complete a purchase, offering guest checkout options, and providing clear instructions and prompts throughout the process.

Furthermore, implementing SSL (Secure Sockets Layer) encryption on your website is essential to protect sensitive customer information, such as credit card details and personal data, from unauthorized access or interception by malicious third parties. SSL encryption encrypts data transmitted between the customer's web browser and your website, ensuring that it remains secure and confidential.

In addition to security measures, offering multiple payment methods can enhance the shopping experience for your customers and cater to their preferences. While credit and debit card payments are standard, consider supporting alternative payment methods, such as digital wallets (e.g., Apple Pay, Google Pay), bank transfers, or even cryptocurrency payments, to accommodate diverse customer preferences and increase conversion rates.

Moreover, providing transparent pricing and shipping information upfront can help reduce cart abandonment rates and build trust with your customers. Clearly display product prices, taxes, shipping costs, and delivery options during the checkout process to eliminate surprises and ensure a smooth purchasing experience.

To further enhance the payment experience for your customers, consider implementing features such as automatic recurring billing for subscription-based services or installment payment options for larger purchases. These features can provide flexibility and convenience for customers while also increasing customer loyalty and retention.

Lastly, regularly monitor and analyze your online store's payment performance to identify any issues or areas for improvement. Track key metrics such as transaction success rates, average order value, and customer churn rates to gain insights into your store's payment processes and identify opportunities for optimization.

By selecting the right website builder, integrating a reliable payment gateway, and optimizing your checkout process, you can create a secure and efficient payment system for your online store.

Providing a seamless payment experience for your customers not only enhances their satisfaction but also contributes to the overall success and growth of your e-commerce business.

CHAPTER 11 - VIRTUAL OFFICE SETUP

Embracing the Virtual Workspace Concept

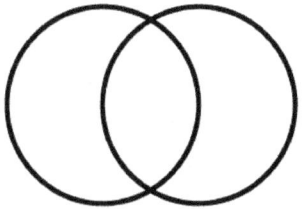

Embracing the virtual workspace concept has been a game-changer for me and my business. It's a paradigm shift from the traditional brick-and-mortar office setup to a more flexible, efficient, and accessible way of working. As someone who values flexibility and autonomy, transitioning to a virtual workspace has allowed me to redefine how I approach work and has opened up a world of opportunities.

One of the most significant advantages of embracing the virtual workspace concept is the freedom it affords. No longer bound by the constraints of a physical office, I can work from anywhere in the world as long as I have an internet connection. Whether it's from the comfort of my home, a bustling coffee shop, or a serene beach destination, I have the flexibility to choose my ideal workspace based on my preferences and needs.

Another benefit of the virtual workspace is the ability to tap into a global talent pool. With remote work becoming increasingly common, businesses can recruit top talent from around the world without being limited by geographical boundaries. This allows for greater diversity and expertise within the team, leading to more innovative ideas and solutions.

Moreover, the virtual workspace promotes a healthier work-life balance. By eliminating the need for a daily commute and offering more flexibility in scheduling, remote work enables me to better prioritize my personal and professional commitments. I have more time to spend with my family, pursue hobbies and interests, and take care of my well-being, ultimately leading to greater overall satisfaction and fulfillment.

In addition to the personal benefits, embracing the virtual workspace concept also has significant advantages for businesses. It reduces overhead costs associated with maintaining a physical office, such as rent, utilities, and office supplies. This allows businesses to allocate resources more efficiently and invest in areas that drive growth and innovation while enhancing employee productivity and engagement.

Studies have shown that remote workers tend to be more productive and satisfied with their jobs compared to their office-bound counterparts. The flexibility to work during their most productive hours, customize their workspace, and avoid office distractions contributes to higher levels of focus and motivation.

Of course, embracing the virtual workspace concept is not without its challenges. Communication and collaboration can be more challenging in a virtual environment, requiring intentional efforts to foster connection and camaraderie among team members. Additionally, maintaining a sense of work-life balance can be difficult when the boundaries between work and home life blur.

However, with the right mindset, tools, and strategies in place, these challenges can be overcome. By leveraging technology platforms for communication and collaboration, establishing clear expectations and boundaries, and prioritizing employee well-being, businesses can create a thriving virtual workspace that benefits both individuals and the organization as a whole.

Embracing the virtual workspace concept offers numerous advantages for individuals and businesses alike. From greater flexibility and autonomy to cost savings and productivity gains, the virtual workspace has transformed the way we work and has become an integral part of the modern work environment. By embracing this shift and adapting to the changing landscape of work, we can unlock new opportunities for growth, innovation, and success.

Essential Tools and Technologies for Remote Work

Transitioning to remote work requires the right tools and technologies to ensure seamless communication, collaboration, and productivity. Over the years, I've experimented with various tools and platforms to create an effective virtual workspace that allows me to work efficiently from anywhere in the world. Here are some essential tools and technologies for remote work that I've found invaluable:

1. **Communication Tools:** Effective communication is the cornerstone of remote work. Platforms like Slack, Microsoft Teams, or Discord provide real-time messaging, video conferencing, and file sharing capabilities, allowing team members to stay connected and collaborate effortlessly. These tools facilitate quick discussions, project updates, and brainstorming ses-

sions, fostering a sense of camaraderie and teamwork despite physical distance.

2. **Project Management Software:** Managing tasks and projects remotely requires robust project management software. Tools like Asana, Trello, or Monday.com offer features such as task assignment, progress tracking, and deadline management, enabling teams to stay organized and focused on their goals. With clear project timelines, priorities, and responsibilities, remote teams can ensure that projects are completed on time and within budget.

3. **Cloud Storage Solutions:** Storing and accessing files securely is essential for remote teams. Cloud storage solutions like Google Drive, Dropbox, or OneDrive provide a centralized platform for storing, syncing, and sharing files across devices. With cloud storage, team members can collaborate on documents in real time, access files from anywhere, and maintain version control, eliminating the need for cumbersome email attachments or USB drives.

4. **Virtual Private Network (VPN):** Protecting sensitive data and ensuring privacy is paramount in remote work. A VPN encrypts internet traffic, providing a secure connection to corporate networks and preventing unauthorized access to confidential information. Whether working from a coffee shop or a co-working space, a VPN ensures that remote workers can access company resources safely and securely.

5. **Time Tracking Software:** Tracking billable hours and monitoring productivity is essential for remote workers. Time tracking software like Toggl, Harvest, or Clockify allows individuals to log their time spent on various tasks and projects accurately. This not only helps with client billing and project management but also enables individuals to identify time-wasting activities and optimize their workflow for maximum efficiency.
6. **Virtual Meeting Platforms:** Hosting virtual meetings and presentations is a common occurrence in remote work. Platforms like Zoom, GoToMeeting, or Webex offer features such as video conferencing, screen sharing, and webinar capabilities, making it easy to conduct meetings with colleagues, clients, or stakeholders regardless of their location. These tools enhance collaboration and communication, facilitating productive discussions and decision-making.
7. **Remote Desktop Software:** Accessing office computers or servers remotely may be necessary for certain tasks or applications. Remote desktop software like TeamViewer, AnyDesk, or Remote Desktop Protocol (RDP) allows users to connect to their work computers from anywhere with an internet connection. This enables remote workers to access files, applications, and resources as if they were physically present in the office, enhancing productivity and flexibility.
8. **Cybersecurity Solutions:** Protecting against cyber threats is essential in remote work environments. An-

tivirus software, firewalls, and endpoint protection tools help safeguard devices and networks from malware, phishing attacks, and other security risks. Additionally, employee training and awareness programs educate remote workers about cybersecurity best practices and mitigate the risk of human error.

9. **Collaborative Document Editing:** Collaborating on documents in real time is crucial for remote teams. Platforms like Google Docs, Microsoft Office Online, or Notion allow multiple users to edit documents simultaneously, track changes, and leave comments. This fosters collaboration and streamlines the document review process, ensuring that everyone is working from the latest version of a document.
10. **Task Automation Tools:** Automating repetitive tasks can save time and increase efficiency for remote workers. Tools like Zapier, IFTTT, MerlinMagic.ai, or Automate.io allow users to create workflows that automate routine tasks, such as sending email reminders, updating spreadsheets, or posting social media updates. By eliminating manual processes, remote workers can focus on more high-value tasks and improve their overall productivity.

Leveraging the right tools and technologies is essential for success in remote work. From communication and collaboration platforms to project management software and cybersecurity solutions, investing in the right tools can enhance productivity, efficiency, and effectiveness in a virtual workspace. By embracing these essential tools and adapting to the demands of remote work, individuals and organizations can thrive in an increasingly digital and interconnected world.

Ensuring Productivity and Collaboration Online

Ensuring productivity and fostering collaboration in an online work environment are essential for remote teams to thrive. Over the years, I've learned valuable strategies and techniques to promote productivity and collaboration among team members, even when working from different locations.

Setting clear goals and expectations is crucial for remote teams to stay focused and aligned. Clearly define project objectives, timelines, and deliverables to provide clarity on what needs to be accomplished and encourage open communication and transparency to ensure that everyone understands their role and responsibilities within the team.

Always use agile methodologies, such as Scrum or Kanban, to provide a framework for iterative and collaborative project management. Break down projects into manageable tasks or user stories, prioritize them based on importance and urgency, and track progress using visual boards or digital tools. Daily stand-up meetings or check-ins allow team members to discuss their progress, share updates, and address any challenges or blockers.

Managing time effectively is crucial for remote workers to maintain productivity and avoid distractions. Encourage team members to use time management techniques such as the Pomodoro Technique, time blocking, or the Eisenhower Matrix to prioritize tasks, allocate time efficiently, and maintain focus. Set realistic deadlines and milestones to keep projects on track and prevent procrastination.

Remote work can blur the boundaries between work and personal life, leading to burnout and decreased productivity. Encourage team members to take regular breaks, stretch, and disconnect from work to recharge and rejuvenate. Encouraging a healthy work-life balance and promoting employee well-being are essential for long-term productivity and job satisfaction.

Utilizing collaboration tools and platforms is essential for remote teams to communicate effectively and work together seamlessly. Platforms like Slack, Microsoft Teams, or Discord provide real-time messaging, file sharing, and video conferencing capabilities, allowing team members to collaborate regardless of their location. Shared documents, wikis, and knowledge bases facilitate information sharing and collaboration on projects.

Promote Transparent Communication for remote teams to build trust, resolve conflicts, and foster collaboration. Encourage team members to communicate openly about their progress, challenges, and ideas. Regular team meetings, one-on-one check-ins, and virtual coffee chats provide opportunities for team members to connect, share updates, and address any issues or concerns.

Establish remote work policies and guidelines to help set expectations and ensure consistency across the team. Define working hours, communication protocols, and response times to provide clarity on when team members are expected to be available and responsive. Encourage flexibility and autonomy while maintaining accountability and professionalism in remote work practices.

Remote work may require individuals to adapt to new tools, technologies, and workflows. Provide adequate training and support to help team members navigate remote work challenges and maximize their productivity. Offer resources, tutorials, and peer mentoring to empower team members to develop the skills and confidence needed to succeed in a virtual work environment.

Always recognize and celebrate achievements, milestones, and successes to boost morale and motivate remote teams. Acknowledge individual and team accomplishments, whether big or small, and express appreciation for their contributions. Virtual celebrations, team awards, and shout-outs in team meetings help foster a positive and supportive work culture, even in a remote setting.

Ask for feedback from team members and stakeholders in order to identify areas for improvement and driving continuous growth and development. Conduct regular retrospectives or feedback sessions to reflect on past projects, discuss lessons learned, and identify opportunities for improvement. Encourage a culture of continuous learning, experimentation, and adaptation to drive innovation and success in remote work.

Overcoming Challenges of Remote Operations

In the world of remotely operated businesses, surmounting challenges is pivotal to ensuring the triumph and endurance of virtual work environments. While remote work boasts myriad advantages, it also presents distinctive hurdles that necessitate resolution to uphold productivity, collaboration, and employee welfare.

Among the challenges of remote operations are communication barriers. Absent face-to-face interaction, team members may encounter difficulties in conveying tone, intention, or context effectively, leading to misunderstandings or miscommunication. To surmount this challenge, employ a spectrum of communication channels such as video conferencing, instant messaging, and email to facilitate clear and transparent communication. Foster active listening, prompt clarifying inquiries, and offer regular updates to ensure seamless information dissemination among team members.

Remote work can also precipitate feelings of isolation and loneliness, particularly for employees accustomed to traditional office settings. Devoid of the social interactions and camaraderie endemic to office environments, remote workers may experience detachment or loneliness vis-à-vis their colleagues. To counteract this challenge, prioritize opportunities for virtual team bonding activities such as virtual coffee chats, team-building exercises, or online social events. Encourage informal communication and collaboration to nurture a sense of belonging and community among remote team members.

Encourage maintaining a harmonious work-life balance to avert burnout and preserve overall well-being. Nevertheless, remote work may blur the demarcation between professional and personal life, rendering it arduous for employees to disengage and recharge. To foster work-life equilibrium, delineate distinct boundaries between work hours and personal time, advocate for regular breaks and screen-free intervals, and furnish resources and support for managing stress and mental health. Encourage employees to prioritize self-care and establish realistic expectations for workload and availability.

Technical glitches and connectivity snags can disrupt remote work operations and impede productivity. Inadequate internet connectivity, software malfunctions, or hardware breakdowns may hinder employees' access to crucial tools or impede effective collaboration with team members. To mitigate these challenges, furnish reliable technology infrastructure and support for remote workers, encompassing access to high-speed internet, dependable software and hardware, and technical assistance as required. Encourage employees to troubleshoot common tech issues autonomously and furnish resources or training to equip them with the acumen to surmount technical obstacles effectively.

Effectively managing remote teams necessitates adept leadership, communication, and collaboration skills. Lacking physical proximity, managers may grapple with furnishing guidance, support, and feedback to remote team members. To surmount this hurdle, concentrate on cultivating trust, transparency, and accountability within the team. Establish explicit expectations, goals, and performance metrics for remote employees, and furnish regular feedback and accolades for their contributions. Foster open communication and collaboration through routine check-ins, team meetings, and project updates to sustain alignment and engagement among remote teams.

Remote teams may encompass members hailing from diverse cultural backgrounds or time zones, engendering challenges related to communication, collaboration, and workflow synchronization. Cultural disparities in communication styles, work practices, or expectations may necessitate sensitivity and awareness to ensure effective collaboration and teamwork.

Similarly, managing teams spanning multiple time zones demands meticulous planning and coordination to accommodate varied schedules and availability. To address these challenges, propagate cultural awareness and sensitivity within the team, institute flexible work hours or meeting times to accommodate diverse time zones, and harness technology tools and platforms to facilitate collaboration across geographical boundaries.

By proactively addressing these challenges and implementing effective strategies for communication, collaboration, and support, organizations can surmount the impediments of remote operations and cultivate a flourishing virtual work environment. Embracing flexibility, adaptability, and resilience is indispensable for navigating the complexities of remote work successfully and attaining enduring prosperity in virtual operations.

CHAPTER 12 - PERFORMANCE MONITORING AND ANALYTICS

The importance of monitoring performance

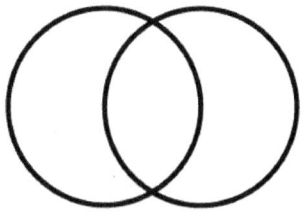

Monitoring performance is a critical aspect of managing any website or online business. It provides valuable insights into how well your website is performing, identifies areas for improvement, and helps you make informed decisions to optimize your online presence. As someone deeply invested in the success of my online ventures, I've learned firsthand the importance of monitoring performance and leveraging data to drive continuous improvement.

One of the primary reasons why monitoring performance is crucial is that it allows you to track the effectiveness of your online strategies and initiatives. Whether you're running marketing campaigns, launching new products, or implementing website changes, monitoring performance enables you to measure the impact of these efforts and determine their success. Without proper monitoring, you're essentially operating in the dark, unable to gauge the effectiveness of your actions or identify areas that require attention.

Furthermore, monitoring performance provides valuable insights into user behavior and preferences. By analyzing metrics such as website traffic, bounce rates, and conversion rates, you can gain a deeper understanding of how users interact with your website and identify opportunities for improvement. For example, if you notice a high bounce rate on a particular page, it may indicate that the content or user experience needs to be optimized to better engage visitors and encourage them to explore further.

Another key benefit of monitoring performance is that it helps you identify and address issues promptly. Whether it's a technical glitch, a drop in website traffic, or a decline in conversion rates, monitoring performance allows you to detect anomalies or discrepancies early on and take corrective action before they escalate into more significant problems. This proactive approach can help minimize downtime, mitigate potential losses, and maintain the integrity and reliability of your online presence.

Moreover, monitoring performance enables you to set benchmarks and track progress over time. By establishing key performance indicators (KPIs) and regularly monitoring relevant metrics, you can track your performance against established goals and objectives. This not only helps you measure the effectiveness of your strategies but also provides valuable insights into areas where you're excelling and areas where you may need to course-correct.

In today's competitive online landscape, where success is often determined by data-driven decision-making, monitoring performance is no longer optional, it's essential. By leveraging the wealth of data available through analytics tools and platforms, you can gain actionable insights into your website's performance, user behavior, and overall online effectiveness. Whether you're a small business owner, an e-commerce entrepreneur, or a digital marketer, monitoring performance is a fundamental practice that can drive continuous improvement and ultimately contribute to your online success.

Utilizing Google Analytics for Insights

Utilizing Google Analytics for insights is a game-changer when it comes to understanding your website's performance and user behavior. It's not just about gathering data; it's about gaining actionable insights that can drive strategic decisions and improvements. As someone committed to optimizing the impact of my online presence, I've come to rely on Google Analytics as a powerful tool for gaining valuable insights into my website's performance and user engagement.

Google Analytics offers a wealth of features and capabilities that enable you to track and analyze various aspects of your website's performance. From basic metrics like website traffic and page views to more advanced insights like user demographics and behavior, Google Analytics provides a comprehensive view of how users interact with your website.

One of the key benefits of Google Analytics is its ability to track user behavior across different devices and platforms. Whether your users are accessing your website from a desktop computer, a mobile device, or a tablet, Google Analytics captures valuable data about their browsing habits and preferences. This insight allows you to optimize your website for different devices and ensure a seamless user experience across all platforms.

Additionally, Google Analytics provides valuable information about user acquisition and traffic sources. By analyzing metrics such as referral traffic, organic search, and social media referrals, you can gain insights into where your website traffic is coming from and which channels are driving the most engagement. This information enables you to refine your marketing strategies and allocate resources more effectively to channels that yield the highest return on investment.

Furthermore, Google Analytics offers in-depth insights into user engagement and behavior on your website. You can track metrics such as bounce rate, average session duration, and conversion rates to understand how users interact with your content and navigate through your website. Armed with this information, you can identify areas for improvement, optimize your website's layout and content, and ultimately enhance the overall user experience.

One of the most valuable features of Google Analytics is its ability to track and measure the effectiveness of your marketing campaigns. Whether you're running email campaigns, social media ads, or pay-per-click campaigns, Google Analytics provides valuable insights into campaign performance, including metrics such as click-through rates, conversion rates, and return on investment. This information enables you to refine your marketing strategies, allocate budgets more effectively, and maximize the impact of your marketing efforts.

Google Analytics is an invaluable tool for gaining insights into your website's performance and user behavior. By leveraging its features and capabilities, you can make informed decisions, optimize your website for maximum effectiveness, and drive continuous improvement. Whether you're a seasoned digital marketer or a novice website owner, Google Analytics empowers you to unlock the full potential of your online presence and achieve your business objectives.

Alternative Analytics Tools

While Google Analytics is undoubtedly a powerful and widely used tool for website analytics, there are several alternative analytics tools available that offer unique features and capabilities. I've explored various analytics tools to gain deeper insights into my website's performance and user behavior. Here are some alternative analytics tools that I've found valuable:

1. **Matomo (formerly Piwik):** Matomo is an open-source analytics platform that offers similar features to Google Analytics but with a focus on data privacy and security. With Matomo, you can host the analytics software on your own server, giving you full control over your data. It provides comprehensive insights into website traffic, user behavior, and conversion rates, making it a popular choice for users who prioritize data privacy and ownership.

2. **Mixpanel:** Mixpanel is a user analytics platform that specializes in tracking and analyzing user interactions with web and mobile applications. Unlike traditional analytics tools that focus on page views and sessions, Mixpanel offers event-based tracking, allowing you to monitor specific user actions and behaviors. This enables you to gain deeper insights into user engagement, retention, and conversion funnels, making it ideal for businesses with complex user journeys.
3. **Adobe Analytics:** Adobe Analytics is a robust analytics solution that offers enterprise-level features and capabilities for tracking and analyzing digital marketing efforts. It provides advanced segmentation and reporting tools, real-time data analysis, and integration with other Adobe marketing solutions. With Adobe Analytics, you can gain a comprehensive understanding of customer behavior across multiple channels and touchpoints, enabling you to optimize your marketing strategies and drive business growth.
4. **Hotjar:** Hotjar is a user behavior analytics and feedback tool that helps you understand how users interact with your website through heatmaps, session recordings, and feedback polls. It provides visual insights into user behavior, allowing you to identify areas for improvement and optimize the user experience. With features like heatmaps and session recordings, Hotjar enables you to see exactly how users nav-

igate your website, where they click, and how they interact with your content.

5. **Clicky**: Clicky is a real-time web analytics tool that offers intuitive dashboards and easy-to-understand reports for tracking website traffic and user behavior. It provides real-time data on website visitors, including their location, device, and referral source. Clicky also offers heatmaps, conversion tracking, and goal tracking features to help you understand user engagement and conversion paths. With its user-friendly interface and real-time monitoring capabilities, Clicky is a popular choice for website owners who value simplicity and ease of use.

While Google Analytics is a dominant force in the world of website analytics, there are several alternative analytics tools available that offer unique features and capabilities to suit different needs and preferences. Whether you prioritize data privacy, user behavior analysis, or real-time monitoring, there's an analytics tool out there that can help you gain deeper insights into your website's performance and drive continuous improvement. By exploring these alternative analytics tools, you can find the right solution for your specific needs and take your website analytics to the next level.

Key Performance Indicators (KPIs)

Let's delve into the world of KPIs and unlock the secrets to online success. Imagine you're embarking on a road trip to your dream destination. You have a map, but without milestones and markers along the way, how would you know if you're on the right track or if you've reached your destination? That's where KPIs come in, they're like signposts guiding you towards your goals in the vast landscape of the online world.

So, what exactly are KPIs? Think of them as measurable values that indicate how effectively you're achieving your key business objectives. Just like in our road trip analogy, KPIs help you track progress, make informed decisions, and stay focused on your ultimate destination, success.

Now, let's break down the concept of KPIs into simpler terms. Imagine you're running an online store selling handmade crafts. Your main goal is to increase sales and grow your business. But how do you measure if you're making progress towards that goal? This is where KPIs come into play.

For your online store, some key performance indicators might include:

1. **Conversion Rate:** This KPI measures the percentage of website visitors who make a purchase. A higher conversion rate indicates that your website is effec-

tively turning visitors into customers, driving revenue growth.
2. **Average Order Value (AOV):** AOV is the average amount spent by customers on each purchase. Tracking AOV helps you understand buying patterns and identify opportunities to increase sales by encouraging customers to spend more per transaction.
3. **Customer Acquisition Cost (CAC):** CAC measures how much it costs to acquire a new customer. By comparing CAC to customer lifetime value (CLV), you can determine if your marketing efforts are generating a positive return on investment (ROI).
4. **Website Traffic:** This KPI tracks the number of visitors to your website over a specific period. Increasing website traffic can lead to higher visibility, brand awareness, and potential sales opportunities.
5. **Customer Satisfaction (CSAT):** CSAT measures the level of satisfaction among your customers. By collecting feedback through surveys or reviews, you can gauge how well your products and services meet customer expectations and identify areas for improvement.
6. **Cart Abandonment Rate:** This KPI measures the percentage of users who add items to their shopping cart but leave the website without completing the purchase. A high cart abandonment rate may indicate issues with the checkout process or pricing, requiring optimization to improve conversion rates.

Now, let's put these KPIs into action with our online store example. Imagine you notice a decline in conversion rates and an increase in cart abandonment rates. This signals potential issues in the purchasing process, such as a complicated checkout process or unexpected shipping costs. By identifying these trends through KPIs, you can take corrective action, such as streamlining the checkout process or offering free shipping incentives, to improve the overall shopping experience and boost sales.

In addition to these quantitative KPIs, it's also essential to consider qualitative factors that contribute to online success. These may include brand reputation, customer loyalty, and engagement metrics such as social media interactions and email open rates. While these metrics may be more challenging to measure, they provide valuable insights into the overall health and perception of your business.

Ultimately, the key to leveraging KPIs for online success lies in setting clear goals, selecting relevant metrics, and regularly monitoring performance to identify trends and opportunities for improvement. By using KPIs as your guiding compass, you can navigate the ever-changing landscape of the online world with confidence and drive your business towards greater heights of success.

Iterative Improvements Based on Data Analysis

Iterative improvements based on data analysis are the cornerstone of continuous optimization in the digital realm. Imagine you're a sculptor crafting a masterpiece out of marble. Each chisel and stroke of the hammer refines the sculpture, bringing it closer to perfection. Similarly, in the world of online business, data analysis serves as your chisel, allowing you to sculpt your digital presence into a finely tuned work of art.

So, what exactly do I mean by iterative improvements? Well, it's all about the process of making incremental changes to your website, marketing strategies, and overall online presence based on insights gleaned from data analysis. Rather than relying on gut feelings or guesswork, iterative improvements empower you to make informed decisions backed by concrete evidence.

Let's break down the iterative improvement process into manageable steps:

1. **Collecting Data:** The first step in iterative improvements is gathering data from various sources, such as website analytics, customer feedback, and market research. This data provides valuable insights into user behavior, preferences, and trends, serving as the foundation for informed decision-making.

2. **Analyzing Data:** Once you've collected data, the next step is to analyze it to identify patterns, trends, and areas for improvement. Tools like Google Analytics, heatmaps, and A/B testing platforms can help you uncover valuable insights about your website performance, user engagement, and conversion rates.
3. **Identifying Opportunities:** With data analysis in hand, you can pinpoint specific areas of your online presence that could benefit from optimization. This might include tweaking website design elements, refining marketing campaigns, or enhancing product offerings based on customer feedback.
4. **Implementing Changes:** Once you've identified opportunities for improvement, it's time to take action. Implement changes to your website, marketing strategies, or business processes based on the insights gained from data analysis. This might involve redesigning landing pages, updating product descriptions, or adjusting pricing strategies to better align with customer preferences.
5. **Measuring Impact:** After implementing changes, it's crucial to monitor their impact on key performance metrics. Use data analytics tools to track changes in website traffic, conversion rates, and other relevant KPIs to assess the effectiveness of your improvements.
6. **Iterating and Refining:** The iterative improvement process doesn't end with a single round of changes. Instead, it's an ongoing cycle of refinement and opti-

mization. Continuously monitor performance metrics, gather feedback from users, and iterate on your strategies to drive continuous improvement over time.

By embracing the iterative improvement mindset, you can adapt to changing market dynamics, respond to customer needs, and stay ahead of the competition in the fast-paced digital landscape. Remember, Rome wasn't built in a day, and neither is online success. But with patience, perseverance, and a commitment to data-driven decision-making, you can sculpt your digital presence into a masterpiece that stands the test of time.

Strategies for Continuous Optimization

Continuous optimization is the heartbeat of any successful online venture. It's the process of fine-tuning your digital presence to maximize performance, enhance user experience, and drive sustainable growth over time. Just like a well-oiled machine, your online business requires regular maintenance and optimization to ensure it operates at peak efficiency. In this section, we'll explore some strategies for continuous optimization that will help you stay ahead of the curve in the ever-evolving digital landscape.

1. **Set Clear Goals and Objectives**: Before diving into optimization efforts, it's essential to define clear goals

and objectives for your online business. Whether you're aiming to increase website traffic, boost conversion rates, or improve customer engagement, having specific, measurable goals will provide direction for your optimization strategies.

2. **Regularly Monitor Key Performance Metrics:** Keep a close eye on key performance indicators (KPIs) relevant to your business objectives. These may include metrics such as website traffic, conversion rates, bounce rates, average session duration, and customer acquisition costs. By regularly monitoring KPIs, you can quickly identify areas that require optimization and measure the impact of your efforts over time.

3. **Utilize A/B Testing and Experimentation:** A/B testing, also known as split testing, allows you to compare two or more versions of a webpage, email, or advertisement to determine which performs better. By testing different elements such as headlines, call-to-action buttons, and layout variations, you can gather valuable data about user preferences and optimize your content for maximum effectiveness.

4. **Optimize Website Performance and User Experience:** Website speed and usability play a crucial role in user satisfaction and search engine rankings. Optimize your website for speed by minimizing page load times, optimizing images and multimedia content, and leveraging caching and content delivery networks (CDNs). Additionally, focus on improving user experience by ensuring intuitive navigation, mobile

responsiveness, and clear calls-to-action throughout your site.

5. **Invest in Search Engine Optimization (SEO):** SEO is essential for driving organic traffic to your website and improving its visibility in search engine results pages (SERPs). Conduct keyword research to identify relevant search terms and optimize your website content, meta tags, and backlink profile accordingly. Regularly update and refresh your content to keep it relevant and engaging for both users and search engines.

6. **Stay Abreast of Industry Trends and Best Practices:** The digital landscape is constantly evolving, with new technologies, trends, and best practices emerging regularly. Stay informed about industry developments by reading blogs, attending webinars, and participating in relevant forums and communities. By staying ahead of the curve, you can identify new opportunities for optimization and adapt your strategies to meet changing consumer preferences.

7. **Listen to Customer Feedback:** Your customers are a valuable source of insights into how you can improve your products, services, and overall user experience. Encourage feedback through surveys, social media, and customer support channels, and use this feedback to inform your optimization efforts. Addressing customer concerns and pain points will not only improve satisfaction but also drive loyalty and repeat business.

8. **Embrace Data-Driven Decision-Making**: Base your optimization strategies on data rather than assumptions or gut feelings. Use analytics tools to track user behavior, monitor website performance, and measure the impact of your optimization efforts. Analyze this data to identify patterns, trends, and areas for improvement, and use it to inform future optimization strategies.

By implementing these strategies for continuous optimization, you can ensure that your online business remains competitive, relevant, and successful in today's fast-paced internet landscape. Remember that optimization is an ongoing process, and staying proactive and adaptive is key to long-term success.

Analytics for Security Monitoring

While analytics tools are often associated with measuring website performance and user engagement, they can also play a crucial role in monitoring security threats and protecting your online assets. In this section, we'll explore how analytics can be leveraged for security monitoring and threat detection, helping you safeguard your website and sensitive data from potential cyber threats.

Many analytics platforms offer real-time alerting features that can notify you immediately of any suspicious or anomalous activity on your website. By setting up custom alerts based on predefined criteria, such as unusual spikes in traffic, unauthorized access attempts, or suspicious user behavior, you can quickly detect and respond to potential security threats before they escalate.

Analytics tools can analyze historical data and user patterns to identify anomalies or deviations from normal behavior. By establishing baseline metrics for website traffic, user activity, and other key indicators, you can detect unusual patterns or outliers that may indicate a security breach or cyberattack. Automated anomaly detection algorithms can help flag suspicious activity for further investigation, allowing you to take proactive measures to mitigate potential risks.

Analytics can also provide valuable insights into user authentication and access control mechanisms, helping you identify potential vulnerabilities and weaknesses in your security protocols. By analyzing login attempts, user authentication patterns, and access permissions, you can detect unauthorized access attempts or suspicious login activity that may indicate a security threat. Implementing multi-factor authentication, strong password policies, and regular user access reviews can help enhance security and prevent unauthorized access to your website and sensitive data.

Analytics tools often include robust event logging and auditing capabilities that allow you to track and monitor user activities, system events, and security-related incidents in real-time. By maintaining detailed logs of user interactions, system changes, and security events, you can trace the source of security incidents, investigate security breaches, and conduct forensic analysis to identify the root cause of security incidents. Regularly reviewing and analyzing audit logs can help detect and mitigate security threats more effectively, allowing you to take proactive measures to protect your website and data.

Many analytics platforms offer integrations with third-party security solutions and services, allowing you to enhance your security monitoring capabilities and automate threat detection and response processes. By integrating analytics with security information and event management (SIEM) systems, intrusion detection and prevention systems (IDPS), and threat intelligence platforms, you can correlate security events, identify emerging threats, and automate incident response workflows. These integrations enable you to leverage the power of analytics to strengthen your cybersecurity posture and defend against evolving cyber threats effectively.

Analytics can also help organizations ensure compliance with regulatory requirements and industry standards by monitoring key security metrics and generating compliance reports. By tracking security-related KPIs, audit trails, and access controls, you can demonstrate adherence to data protection regulations such as GDPR, HIPAA, PCI DSS, and others. Analytics tools can generate comprehensive compliance reports, facilitate regulatory audits, and provide insights into areas that require remediation or improvement to maintain compliance.

Analytics tools offer powerful capabilities for security monitoring and threat detection, enabling organizations to proactively identify and mitigate security risks, protect sensitive data, and maintain compliance with regulatory requirements. By leveraging analytics for security monitoring, you can enhance your cybersecurity posture, strengthen your defenses against cyber threats, and safeguard your online assets and reputation.

Monitoring performance conclusion

In conclusion, monitoring performance is not just a routine task but a critical aspect of maintaining a successful online presence. Through the insights gained from analytics tools, businesses can make informed decisions, optimize their strategies, and drive continuous improvement across all aspects of their digital operations.

By embracing the virtual workspace concept, adopting essential tools and technologies for remote work, and ensuring productivity and collaboration online, organizations can effectively navigate the challenges of remote operations and maximize efficiency and effectiveness.

Furthermore, implementing robust security measures, leveraging alternative analytics tools, and monitoring key performance indicators (KPIs) for online success are essential steps in safeguarding against cyber threats, ensuring data protection, and maintaining regulatory compliance.

Through iterative improvements based on data analysis, strategies for continuous optimization, and proactive security monitoring, businesses can stay ahead of the curve, adapt to changing market dynamics, and achieve sustainable growth and success in the digital age.

In essence, monitoring performance is not just about tracking numbers or metrics, it's about gaining valuable insights, identifying opportunities for improvement, and driving meaningful outcomes. By embracing a data-driven approach to performance monitoring and analytics, organizations can unlock their full potential, drive innovation, and achieve their goals in today's dynamic and competitive landscape.

CHAPTER 13 - CONCLUSION

Recap of Key Learnings

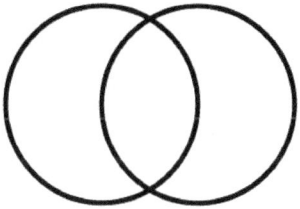

As we near the conclusion of our journey through the realm of online magic, it's essential to reflect on the myriad lessons learned and insights gained. Throughout this comprehensive exploration, we've delved into the intricacies of crafting a successful online presence, from the foundational elements to advanced strategies. Now, let's take a moment to recap the key learnings that can guide us towards sustained success in the digital domain.

1. **Understanding the Importance of a Website**: At the heart of any successful online venture lies a well-designed, purpose-driven website. It serves as the cornerstone of your digital identity, offering a platform

for engagement, interaction, and conversion. By recognizing the pivotal role of your website, you lay the groundwork for building a robust online presence.

2. **Audience Analysis and Content Strategy**: Central to the success of any website is its ability to resonate with its target audience. Through meticulous audience analysis and the development of a tailored content strategy, you can ensure that your digital offerings align seamlessly with the needs, preferences, and aspirations of your visitors. Crafting compelling content and calls-to-action forms the bedrock of user engagement and conversion.

3. **Design and User Experience Optimization**: Aesthetics and functionality go hand in hand in the digital realm. By prioritizing user-centric design principles and optimizing the overall user experience, you create a welcoming and intuitive environment for visitors. From seamless navigation to visually striking aesthetics, every aspect of your website should be meticulously crafted to delight and engage users.

4. **Website Maintenance and Security**: The digital landscape is constantly evolving, necessitating ongoing maintenance and vigilant security measures. Regular updates, backups, and security protocols are essential for safeguarding your website against cyber threats and ensuring uninterrupted functionality. By prioritizing website maintenance and security, you demonstrate your commitment to providing a safe and reliable online experience for your audience.

5. **Marketing Strategies and Monetization Tactics**: A well-executed marketing strategy is indispensable for driving traffic, generating leads, and maximizing revenue. From harnessing the power of search engine optimization (SEO) to leveraging social media and traditional marketing channels, the possibilities for promoting your website are vast and varied. Similarly, exploring diverse monetization methods, from Google AdWords to affiliate programs, can unlock new avenues for generating income and expanding your digital footprint.
6. **Embracing the Virtual Workspace**: In an increasingly interconnected world, the concept of the virtual office has emerged as a viable alternative to traditional workspaces. By embracing remote work tools and technologies, you can create a flexible and dynamic work environment that transcends geographical boundaries. From enhancing collaboration to fostering productivity, the virtual office offers myriad benefits for modern businesses and professionals alike.
7. **Performance Monitoring and Analytics**: Data-driven insights are indispensable for optimizing your online presence and driving continuous improvement to your website. By leveraging tools such as Google Analytics and monitoring key performance indicators (KPIs), you gain valuable insights into user behavior, website performance, and overall effectiveness. Armed with this knowledge, you can refine your on-

line strategies, identify areas for growth, and adapt to evolving market dynamics.

Encouragement for Ongoing Development

Dear Readers,

Congratulations on taking the significant step of establishing your online presence through the creation of your website. Now that your digital footprint is firmly planted in the vast landscape of the internet, it's essential to nurture and cultivate this virtual extension of yourself or your business with care and dedication.

Think of your website as more than just a collection of web pages, it's a living entity that requires ongoing attention and maintenance. Whether your website serves as a personal portfolio, a showcase for your creative endeavors, or a storefront for your business, it holds immense value and potential.

For those who have built their websites for business purposes, it's crucial to recognize that your website is a direct reflection of your company's image and ethos. Every element of your site, from its design to its content, serves as a testament to your professionalism, credibility, and dedication to quality. As such, it's imperative to ensure that your website conveys the right message to your visitors, leaving a lasting impression that inspires trust and confidence.

When it comes to design, simplicity reigns supreme. Remember the age-old adage, "Keep it simple, stupid" (KISS). Strive for a clean, intuitive design that prioritizes usability and functionality above flashy aesthetics. While visual elements such as artwork and animations can enhance the appeal of your website, exercise restraint to prevent them from overshadowing your core message and objectives.

Maintaining the delicate balance between artistic flair and practicality is key. Aim for a harmonious blend of visual elements and textual content, with a slight emphasis on the latter for optimal search engine visibility. Additionally, leverage animations judiciously, ensuring that they enhance rather than detract from the user experience.

Above all, remember that building a successful website is not a one-time endeavor, it's an ongoing journey of growth, refinement, and adaptation. Stay engaged with your website, regularly updating and optimizing its content, design, and functionality to keep pace with evolving trends and user preferences.

As you embark on this ongoing journey of website development and optimization, embrace the opportunity to learn, experiment, and innovate. Let your website serve as a dynamic reflection of your passion, creativity, and commitment to excellence.

Final Thoughts on Online Magic the True Path to Success

In the expansive and continually shifting terrain of the internet, stories of rapid triumph frequently captivate our imagination and ignite our ambitions. We've all heard the fabled stories of individuals who seemingly struck gold with a single website, skyrocketing to fame and fortune in the blink of an eye. Yet, upon closer examination, we realize that such narratives are but myths, far removed from the realities of building and sustaining a successful online presence.

Undoubtedly, the journey to online success is fraught with challenges, setbacks, and uncertainties. While it's true that building a website is a crucial first step, it's merely the beginning of a long and arduous journey. Contrary to popular belief, success does not materialize overnight; it is the result of perseverance, determination, and unwavering commitment.

Consider the titans of the digital age —Google, Facebook, Twitter, Wikipedia, and countless others— whose meteoric rise to prominence was anything but instantaneous. Behind each success story lies a tale of relentless dedication, tireless effort, and unwavering belief in a vision. These pioneers dared to dream big, defying the odds and overcoming obstacles to carve out their rightful place in the annals of history.

Reflecting on my own journey, I recall the humble beginnings of my first online venture, a fledgling e-commerce company launched from the confines of my own bedroom. Armed with little more than a shoestring budget and boundless ambition, I embarked on a journey fraught with uncertainty and doubt. Yet, through sheer grit and determination, I transformed my vision into reality, building a great company that serves customers across the globe.

However, success did not come without its fair share of challenges. I vividly remember the sleepless nights spent juggling customer inquiries, managing servers, and navigating the intricacies of online commerce. Yet, it was through adversity that I discovered the true power of resilience and resourcefulness.

As I reflect on my journey, I am reminded of the invaluable lessons learned along the way. Chief among them is the importance of embracing a mindset of abundance and possibility. In a world teeming with opportunity, success is not a finite resource reserved for the privileged few, it is a limitless wellspring of potential waiting to be tapped.

In this fast-paced and competitive world, the key to success lies not in passive complacency but in proactive action. Dare to dream big, reach out to potential collaborators and partners, and seize every opportunity with unwavering determination. Remember, success is not bestowed upon the fortunate few, it is earned through perseverance, resilience, and an unyielding commitment to excellence.

As we bid farewell to this exploration of online magic, let us carry forth the lessons learned and insights gained on our journey towards success. Armed with a spirit of resilience, a thirst for knowledge, and an unwavering belief in our potential, we can conquer any challenge and achieve greatness beyond measure.

Here's to the brave souls who dare to dream, the relentless innovators who defy the odds, and the unwavering optimists who believe in the transformative power of online magic. May your journey be filled with boundless opportunities, endless growth, and unparalleled success.

Until we meet again on the digital frontier, keep dreaming, keep striving, and never lose sight of the magic that lies within.

With warmest regards,
Andree Ochoa

GLOSSARY

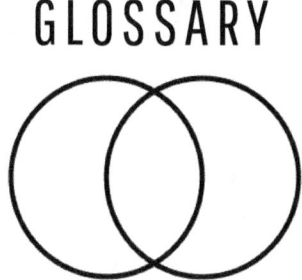

1. **AOV (Average Order Value):** The average amount of money spent by customers in a single transaction on a website.
2. **Anchor Text:** The clickable text in a hyperlink, often used to provide context or describe the linked content.
3. **Back-links:** Links from external websites that direct users to a specific webpage on your website, considered important for SEO.
4. **CAC (Customer Acquisition Cost):** The cost incurred by a business to acquire a new customer.
5. **CDN (Content Delivery Network):** A network of distributed servers that deliver web content to users based on their geographic location, improving website performance and speed.
6. **CLV (Customer Lifetime Value):** The total revenue a business expects to earn from a single customer over the duration of their relationship.

7. **CMS (Content Management System):** A software application or platform that allows users to create, manage, and modify digital content on a website without requiring technical expertise.
8. **CSS (Cascading Style Sheets):** A style sheet language used to define the visual presentation and layout of HTML elements on a webpage.
9. **CTA (Call to Action):** A prompt or directive that encourages users to take a specific action, such as making a purchase, subscribing to a newsletter, or signing up for a service.
10. **DDoS (Distributed Denial of Service):** A cyberattack in which multiple compromised systems are used to flood a targeted website or network with excessive traffic, causing it to become unavailable to legitimate users.
11. **Domain Name:** The unique name that identifies a website on the internet, often used in URLs to access webpages.
12. **HTML (Hypertext Markup Language):** The standard markup language used to create and structure content on webpages.
13. **Hosting:** The service or process of providing storage space and access for websites on servers connected to the internet.
14. **Javascript:** A programming language commonly used to add interactivity and dynamic behavior to webpages.

15. **KPIs (Key Performance Indicators):** Quantifiable metrics used to evaluate the success and performance of a website or digital marketing campaign.
16. **Meta Tags:** HTML tags that provide metadata about a webpage, including information such as page title, description, and keywords.
17. **MFA (Multi-Factor Authentication):** A security mechanism that requires users to provide multiple forms of verification to access an account or system, enhancing security.
18. **PCI DSS (Payment Card Industry Data Security Standard):** Security standards established to protect sensitive payment card data and ensure secure payment transactions.
19. **PHP:** A server-side scripting language commonly used for web development to create dynamic webpages and applications.
20. **PPC (Pay-Per-Click):** An online advertising model in which advertisers pay a fee each time their ad is clicked by a user.
21. **ROI (Return on Investment):** A measure of the profitability or effectiveness of an investment, calculated by dividing the net profit or benefit by the initial investment cost.
22. **RSS Feed:** A web feed that allows users to access and receive updated content from websites in a standardized format.
23. **SEO (Search Engine Optimization):** The process of optimizing a website to improve its visibility and

ranking in search engine results pages (SERPs), leading to increased organic (non-paid) traffic.
24. **SEM (Search Engine Marketing):** A digital marketing strategy that involves promoting websites by increasing their visibility in search engine results pages through paid advertising.
25. **SERPs (Search Engine Results Pages):** The pages displayed by search engines in response to a user's query, containing a list of relevant websites ranked based on their relevance and authority.
26. **SSL (Secure Sockets Layer):** A security protocol that encrypts data transmitted between a user's web browser and a website's server, ensuring secure and private communication.
27. **TLS (Transport Layer Security):** The successor to SSL, TLS is a cryptographic protocol used to secure communications over a computer network.
28. **User-centered design (UCD):** A design approach that prioritizes the needs, preferences, and experiences of users to create intuitive, accessible, and user-friendly products or services.
29. **WAF (Web Application Firewall):** A security system that monitors, filters, and blocks malicious traffic to protect web applications from cyberattacks and vulnerabilities.
30. **Web Content Accessibility Guidelines (WCAG):** A set of guidelines and standards developed to ensure that digital content is accessible to users with disabilities.

31. **Web Traffic:** The amount of data sent and received by visitors to a website, often used as a metric to measure website performance and popularity.
32. **Website:** A collection of webpages and digital content accessible over the internet, typically hosted on a domain name.
33. **WordPress:** A popular open-source content management system (CMS) used to create and manage websites, blogs, and online stores.
34. **XSS (Cross-Site Scripting):** A type of security vulnerability in web applications that allows attackers to inject malicious scripts into webpages viewed by other users.

DISCLAIMER

This publication aims to provide accurate and authoritative information regarding the subject matter covered. It is important to note that, with the exception of Domain-Cart.com, the companies mentioned in this book are referenced solely for illustrative purposes in good faith. The author is not affiliated with these companies. Additionally, the companies referenced herein are owners of their respective trademarks.

The content of this publication is for informational purposes only and should not be construed as professional advice or services. The author and publisher do not accept responsibility for any misuse of the material presented, nor do they assume liability for any loss or damage incurred directly or indirectly from the information provided in this book. It is not guaranteed that individuals who implement the strategies, suggestions, tips, ideas, or techniques outlined in this book will achieve success.

All rights reserved. No part of this book may be reproduced, stored in a retrieval system, or transmitted in any form or by any means, electronic, mechanical, photocopying, recording, or otherwise, without prior written permission from the author. Unauthorized reproduction, distribution, or sharing of this book is prohibited by law. If professional advice or expert assistance is needed, it is recommended to consult with a qualified professional.

www.ingramcontent.com/pod-product-compliance
Lightning Source LLC
Chambersburg PA
CBHW050202230526
45470CB00001B/206